Beyond the Walls

A World All Eyes Can See

T.M. Coal

ISBN 9-780615-379661

Contents

I dedicate this book to the betterment of humanity and thank my parents, my wife, and countless sages, without whom I could not have made this writing.

Introduction

What do you see when you look at the world? Do you see beauty or ugliness? Do you experience joy or sorrow? Do you feel it is possible for us to make the world a better place or do you think it is hopeless? Why do we live? Why do we die? Why do we hurt? Is there any meaning in life?

These questions, and others like them, fill my mind and have done so for many years. With every means available to me I have pursued these questions, and even though I still have much to learn, I have already learned much. I am not a sage or a prophet, I am only a man who has made a life out of asking the questions and doing the things everyone told me not to do.

As a child, this tendency landed me in many bad situations. I was in trouble all the time for questioning authority figures and refusing to conform to the expectations of others. As I grew older however, I began to learn from my mistakes, and with the coming of wisdom my mind turned to life's deepest questions. First, I turned to the religion instilled into me as a child, and did the best I could to comply with all of its requirements. Eventually, I become miserable, things were not happening the way everyone said they should, the world wasn't behaving like it was supposed to, and I determined to find out why.

The path of impartial and critical thought is not popular, nor is it easy, but there is no other path I would suggest or choose. The lessons I have learned, the wisdom I have acquired, and the friends I have made make all hardship seem light and the heaviest of burdens easy to bear.

When I first started to seek the deepest truth, I was convinced I was going to just discover it by the roadside, and then write a book telling everyone all the answers to life's deepest questions. Since then, I have realized every truth is just a door to a room full of questions. When I compare all I know to all that can be known, I am forced to admit I know almost nothing at all. Yet, however small it may be, I want to share it so you might see all the beautiful complexities of life and live it with deep rooted peace.

No matter your age, gender, philosophy, or cultural background, this book is for you. All of us hurt and want to know why, dream and want to build, despair and need the wisdom to know how to rise again. Every human on the earth is beautiful and deserving of love, happiness, and above all truth. When humans realize just how wonderful and powerful they are, they are no longer afraid and can mend not only their wounds but the wounds of our world. Even though pain, violence, and fear fill the earth, beneath them truth waits to guide us to the wisdom we need to forsake fear, obtain healing, and retain peace.

For every hurt there is a cure, and for every aching heart a way to dry the tears. Sometimes, we cannot see the solution because of the walls of ignorance and evil surrounding us, but beyond them lies a world all eyes can see where the wonder is thick like forests and mountains of refuge wait by healing seas to shelter the weary mind. May these words illuminate the path that cannot be fenced, and lead you to glimpse what is beyond all expression.

A Simple Path

Once, a man named Young Man was wondering outside the gates of the city trying to find a place to take some repose from the hustle and bustle of the sleepless throng. Looking up he saw the Mountain, many times he had tried to climb it without success. In fact no one in the history of the city had ever made it to the top. Just at that time he caught a glimpse of a beautiful old woman seated on the peak and singing joyfully. Filled with wonder, he raced up the mountain side as fast as he could, and once he had gone as far as he could go yelled, "How did you get to the top?"

The lady stopped singing, and looking down to see who called, yelled back, "I walked". This was not exactly the answer Young Man was looking for, and so he spoke again, "I figured you walked, but how is it you have made it to the top, a place no one else has ever been?" The lady paused to think for a moment and then called back, "The way was hidden but once I learned how to see correctly it was not hard to find." Young Man had always wanted to see the world from the point closest to heaven so he eagerly asked, "Will you show me the way?" The lady replied, "You too must not know how to see, because it is right in front of you."

Chapter One

As far back into human history as we can see, there have always been those who have sought to find and express the secrets of life. Sages, philosophers, prophets, scholars, poets, scientists, farmers, warriors, parents, lovers, teachers, people from every possible walk of life have tried to share with those around them what they believed to be highest truth.

Every culture has their own system of wisdom teaching them how to understand themselves, others, and the universe we live in. The Greeks used their powers of observation and logic to describe their world and to establish their place in it, while Asia organized itself according to the writings of Buddhist, Taoist and Confucian sages. In the Middle East Islam, Sikhism, and Judaism mold the mind while the various schools of Hindu, Jain, and Buddhist thought give meaning and direct the lives of India's people. Also, we cannot forget how the tribal wisdom of countless native people informed them about the seen and unseen world while helping them to harmonize themselves with nature. In all places and times, people from every area have been asking and answering the biggest and hardest questions life has to offer: Who am I? Where did I come from? Where am I going? How am I to live while I am here in this world?

Even in this age of technological advancement, humanity is still asking these questions, giving their answers, and trying to establish who is right and who is wrong. However, there is one difference between then and now which we cannot overlook; the availability of knowledge.

In our world today, most can find vast amounts of information on anything they care to know with minimal effort. We can buy books once reserved only for those who were ritually pure, socially well put, or descended from the right ancestors. We also have a better understanding of how the mind, body, and the natural world behave than at any other time in recorded history. The secrets of the Universe, and all the information humans have gathered about them, are open to us like never before.

We steep in an ocean of wisdom, insight, and knowledge and what are we doing? We are doing the same evil and useless things that have destroyed our kind for centuries. We fill our minds with worthless information, commit thoughtless acts, teach baseless ideas, and then cry about the difficulties and vices which fill our world. We cherish destructive and outdated ideas, pass them on to others, and then stand awe struck as our world spirals deeper into ignorance and misery.

There are many out there who see the shallowness of the average mind, and the ignorance central to many social ideas and institutions. These people often turn to the systems of wisdom in their culture, and there find the insights into themselves and the world around them which meet their needs. Their thirst quenched, these set about sharing what they have found so others may know their joy.

This is a beautiful thing. However, these new insights often come with the idea the system presenting them is the only correct one. Since there cannot be two versions of truth, this awakens war among systems of wisdom, who otherwise know that fighting seldom deepens understanding or reveals knowledge. All over the world right now families, philosophers, religions, countries, friends, and neighbors are divided and suffering, because those involved think that they or their party have ideas that are totally true, and even a modest alteration of them is only adding corruption to purity.

Conflict is an undeniable part of everyday life, and challenges to our understanding help to keep us sharp and reveal things we may not have seen. However, when the confrontations are not conducted with kindness and respect they do not produce better people, only bitter ones. Lives, happiness, and peace are lost all, because some have been deluded into believing they know everything and insist on everyone else agreeing.

Have we learned nothing from the waste of life and the abuses humans have inflicted upon one another? Are we deaf to history's voice? Bloodshed, violence, and prejudice only create more of themselves. If our wish is to create in the human mind an attitude of love, understanding, and unconditional acceptance, then we must conduct ourselves in this manner. We all know planting apple seeds will give us apples, yet we murder in the name of love, lie for the sake of truth, harm in the name of healing, steal in the name of giving, and then wonder why it is no one is embodying the ideals we claim to profess. This type of behavior is a madness which we all need to rid ourselves of.

There is only one power on earth strong enough to free us from the cage of our preconceptions and desires; the power of wisdom. Wisdom teaches us the value of compassion, compassion leads us to see the value of life, and the value of life teaches how we are to treat ourselves, others, and the world around us. Wisdom also instructs us on how to look at things, how to do things, how to end things, the size of things, and the workings of things. The pupil of wisdom is allowed to live fully in this moment and empowered with the understanding of how to share this style of living. There is no limit to what correct understanding can do when it is mixed with correct action.

What system then shall we turn to in order to learn the ways of wisdom? What path shall we take to get to the place of understanding? We shall take the oldest and most reliable way known to humanity; wisdom itself. Pure wisdom is the only thing that can lead to pure wisdom. Whenever we put names on wisdom, those whom we are trying to teach judge it by its name, and what others have told them this name means. Thus, many have turned away valuable insights. They thought they knew what a system was about when really all they possessed was its name and a bunch of incorrect facts.

It is like a blind taste test in which you are given three boxes of unknown food to try. You do not know what is in the box so you try it, and then your taste buds tell you if it is good or bad. For example, you have the idea in your head that you hate pumpkin pie. To you it is the worst thing on earth and you have sworn to never eat it. You have heard several people, each of whom you deeply respect, say it is filthy and so you *know* it will make you vomit. Yet, a piece of pumpkin pie is in one of the nameless boxes, and once you have tasted it you not only like it, you think it is the best thing you have ever eaten. If you had seen the name *pumpkin pie* on the box, you would never have eaten it. Thus, your ideas about pumpkin pie would have robbed you of its sweet reality.

As it is with pie, so it is with wisdom. Each of us come from a certain religion, culture, mindset, or group and have the prejudices, likes, and dislikes of those around us poured into our head. We each have a certain type of mental food we enjoy, and will only eat it from the boxes carrying the name of the ideas we know and trust; ideas that do not challenge our assumptions or cause us any discomfort. For example, Tuppy, a fundamental Christian, will not consider Jewish ideas because they look bad, will not contemplate Hindu philosophies because they smell funny, and looks upon scientific ideas as poison. Meanwhile, those from other perspectives feel the same way about anything named Christian, so from the start communication is hindered. Yet, by removing the names we can judge the idea based on the flavor and quality of the idea, and not by our preexisting ideas, preferences, or the name on the box.

Names make walls, because they create divisions. Yet, we have to use names so we can communicate to others how we understand the world. Thus, in future chapters I name things based on what they are, and not according to what they are called by any existing system, culture, or way of thinking so communication without bias is more likely.

Another reason I do not use a label more specific than wisdom to title this system, is because there is no title big enough to contain it. Wisdom is universal in size, and to try to put a name on it is like trying to put the universe into a building or the ocean in your belly. Truth and understanding cannot be defined by a single book or system, how much less can it be defined by a word?

Wisdom is infinite in size, because each part is itself endless. Think for a moment only about knowledge, for this is a part of wisdom, and about how many correct facts there are. If humanity put all of its knowledge, past or present, into a book, how long would it be? One person could not write it all down in a lifetime, and all we know is not a fraction of all that could be known. Think about all that was never recorded or has been lost in time, and then add to this all the facts still to be found. One quickly can see how the number of correct facts is almost endless. If the book of knowledge is all but endless, and it is only a part of wisdom, think about how big the whole of wisdom - including compassion, kindness, discipline, temperance, timing, understanding, and right expression - must be?

A good metaphor is to compare life to wisdom. On our earth, how many living things are there? How many different ways are there for a thing to be living and to maintain life? Are bacteria more alive than moths, or can moths judge plants for living wrong? As it is with life, so it is with wisdom - it has millions of forms, is constantly changing, and is more complex than we can comprehend or create.

All the time people ask me, "What do you believe?" To which I reply, "Truth." Then they ask, "What religion is that?", and I reply, "All of them and none of them." Humanity likes to put things into boxes and labels, so we can know how to relate to it and feel as though we understand. However, wisdom is too big for any box, and since I do all I can to live a life reflecting wisdom, I do not allow myself to be put into rigid and lifeless boxes. I reject conventional human systems, because they complicate, limit, and misname wisdom until it is impossible for any to know what it means to be wise.

Wisdom is among the simplest things on earth, yet all the confusing and self-motivated information floating around our world makes it hard for those who just want to live a good life, to know the truth, and to avoid evils. We have millions of voices clamoring for the minds of people, and all of them say they have the highest truth and know the deepest secrets. They say they have what you need, and you must accept it if you ever want to be happy on earth or in any life to come. It is a sad state when the priceless truths that are meant to liberate have tags put on them and drag minds into bondage.

Who owns truth? Which of us created wisdom? Who has the copyright on love and the patent on peace? The answer of course is no one. Happiness, peace, joy, wisdom, beauty, truth, love, healing, and all things akin to them are the inheritance of all those born into the human race. These can be obtained by all who are willing to take the necessary actions, and cannot be sold or possessed by any.

I write this book to make the wonders of wisdom accessible to everyone. To make simple what is often confusing and available what is often odd and hard to read. To show all people the beauty of wisdom, and the power of selfless compassion regardless of their color, class, gender, or creed.

All concepts here in are broken down into their simplest form: truth and lies, peace and chaos, cause and effect, right and wrong. Life's secrets are not confusing in fact they are simple enough for a child to understand. Actually, a child is more likely to understand them, because they have not become filled with social conventions, evil, or themselves, and so they still have room for new understanding and the ability to admit their limits.

Children are a model for all who want to find their way in life; small, humble, unafraid, innocent, curious, full of energy, and free from hope or despair. Children run into the woods and enjoy the wonders adults are too trained to see. Children color outside the lines, dance in the rain, and jump over walls - they are a living illustration of how the seeker is to relate to the endlessness of reality. Let us then take their example and, scurrying over the walls that fetter our minds, begin our adventure in the boundless woods of wisdom.

Ignorance

After Young Man had made his way to the top of the mountain and talked for a while with the woman, named Old Beauty, the two became friends. Young Man realized as non-traditional as she was, she was very fun and deeply wise. Every day, the young man would come and learn from her about nature, about people, and about the art of living.

One day on his way up the mountain, Young Man ate a berry. He was unfamiliar with it, but it was very similar to an edible kind he knew. Since it tasted good, he did not figure it would do him any harm. He arrived at the camp Old Beauty had made at the Mountain's top. She had grown tired of people and decided to live where they could not come, but she liked Young Man's desire to understand, so she did not mind his company. After sitting down and having a cup of tea, the two began to consider what the topic for the day's conversation would be. Suddenly however, Young Man felt his stomach twist just before it spoke, and then running to the bushes he had a most unpleasant experience. Embarrassed, and still suffering with stomach pangs, he started to leave when Old Beauty spoke up, "I see you have chosen today's topic for us". Young Man, though a little puzzled, had become accustomed to Old Beauty's quirkiness, and quietly comforting his angry belly, returned to his seat.

She said sweetly, "You ate the bluish berries because you thought they were similar to blue berries didn't you?" Sheepishly the young man nodded in response as she continued, "Think deeply, you are a living metaphor for ignorance just like the unfortunate ostrich. She thought her darkness was the darkness of the world, she thought herself to be alone because she did not see anyone, and she thought herself powerful because she blotted out the sun. Then, while her head was still in the sand, the lion ate her."

Chapter Two

The first step in rising above the world of suffering, selfishness, and slavery is to face, and fix, our ignorance - our lack of firsthand knowledge, understanding, and experience.

As children, we are given information about how to speak, how to write, and how to read. As we grow, we are given information about what has happened, what should happen, what should not happen, what is going to happen, what to think, and who to trust. By the time we are adults, we have receive so much data and instruction we get the idea we have moved beyond ignorance and into knowledge; nothing could be further from the truth.

Ignorance is like a soft blanket wrapping around the entire earth, and as we grow, its threads are woven into our being. The systems that teach us, the ways we think, and the cultural norms are full of ignorance. We are blind to it because we have become accustomed to it, just as one gets used to the sound of a train or the smell of a house.

As a person who is full will not eat, so those who think they know can never be filled with the wisdom needed to expel ignorance. All improvement and learning come to pass because an individual felt a need or sensed a gap, and sought to fill them. So the first step in improving ourselves is realizing how little it is we really know.

There are some forms of ignorance that are not harmful. For example, if I do not know how a cricket sings, or how a firefly produces its light, my lack of knowledge is not really harmful. However, if I am ignorant in my beliefs, errant in my facts, and wrong in my actions I could end up hating the good, killing the innocent, and refusing the only cure. Even though this is horrible, the greatest horror has yet to be mentioned - I can do all this harm while convinced I am doing what is best.

Almost all spiritual, philosophical, political, and scientific systems understand just how powerful and dangerous ignorance is. The ignorance of the king's subjects keeps them busy merely trying to survive while he controls them. The ignorance of those who seek spiritual truth is used by religious leaders to get their followers to do everything from donations to suicide, and to keep them bound to limited and misinformed views. Ignorance about others causes us to distrust them, and in turn causes intolerance, prejudice, and perversions of justice. Ignorance invariably leads to fear, and fear blinds the mind further, chains the will more, and robs mind of the power to seek anything unknown. Thus, people become forever bound to idiocy.

The amount of harm ignorance causes on a daily basis cannot be overestimated. What we do not know not only hurts us but others as well, and the effects of this hurt spread over the earth like the rays of the rising sun. Ignorance is not the root of all evil, but it is a fertile soil where much evil takes root. Ignorance is an artist that makes unjust, harmful, and depressing things seems attractive, delightful, and good. The problems, heartaches, and consequences created by bad actions and poor choices are hidden to the unlearned mind.

How many would have had the one night stand that led to a lifetime of parenthood or child support, if they knew ahead of time the outcome? How many would have stolen the belongings of another if they knew it would cost them their freedom? How many would have sold drugs if they knew from the start the wake of devastation it would leave in the lives of irresponsible people? How many would have become drunk if they had known a car full of strangers would shortly thereafter die by their hands? It is our lack of knowledge, and laziness of mind causing most of the pain in our world. When we do not think about the consequences of our actions, the truthfulness of our ideas, or how things really are, we awake to find ourselves in a type of hell when we expected heaven. Ignorance must be left behind, and this can only be done by understanding what it is and how it is perpetuated.

Being ignorant - not knowing something - is not the same as being stupid. Ignorance is not a measurement of how smart we are. All of us began life knowing nothing, and through the instruction of others and our own experiences, we have arrived at our current level of understanding. Not knowing something does not make us a fool, it just means we need to learn.

Similarly, one is not wise merely because they have been taught. The systems that inform humanity about what is, what was, and what is to come seldom teach their students to doubt the information they are teaching. You will rarely go into a church, and find the speaker telling his congregation to critically analyze the claims and content of the Bible. Likewise, it is rare to find militant atheists instructing listeners to question their data, or to consider opposing points in a fair and unbiased way. We are not taught how to think, so we might test the truth of all things with logic and wisdom, but rather what to think.

Just because you have been taught by a teacher, a preacher, a guru, a master, a sheikh, or mufti does not mean you know the highest truth of reality. It does mean however, that whatever world view they had, with perhaps some slight modification, has now become yours. This means whatever degree of error and ignorance has infected the system that has taught you truth, to the same degree your understanding of truth is corrupted. This corruption is bad enough, but far worse is the fact not only has truth become corrupted in your mind, your mind now thinks the corruptions themselves are truths of the highest order.

No system of thought on earth has a monopoly on truth. All traditions of wisdom and knowledge are a mix of fact and error; be it error in the texts used to instruct or in the cultural interpretations of those texts. It is for this reason none can be mindlessly loyal to any system, no matter how much it has done for us, how much we cherish it, how many friends and family think it is true, or what joys it may give.

By logic, reflection, research, and comparison we need to scrutinize everything said to be true. Sometimes those we call geniuses and prophets are fools, and sometimes those we call fools are geniuses and prophets. If a thing really is true then inspection of its truthfulness will only it make more apparent. However, if a thing is false then study will make its imperfections clear. Those who are devoted to things and ideas more than they are to truth are the only ones who fear open and objective critical analysis.

Being educated does not necessarily cure ignorance; rather it is the asking of questions, the application of thought, and a personal devotion to truth above all things that rids one of this virus-like quality.

Just as there are different styles of the same virus, so are there different varieties of ignorance. The first variety are those who are ignorant but do not know it. These, like all people, need to be approached in a gentle and kind way by one who is wiser than they are. Then, they might come to see their misconceptions, and start to determine what, if anything, they are going to do about them.

Next, are those who are ignorant but do not care. This group realizes they are living life in a way that is not the best, yet do not care. Some think they are going to live life anyway they want and change when they are old, and then some really believe ignorance is bliss. Regardless of the reason, they need to be approached by one who has wisdom enough to show them no form of ignorance is good, and changing at the end of an unwisely lived life does not undo the harm they have done to themselves or others. What is done can never be undone, thus we cannot afford to blunder along.

Another group is made of those who think they have no ignorance in them, but they are full of it. They have allowed pride and large amounts of study to blind them; knowing some things they have come to believe they know all. By believing they are utterly free from ignorance, they have shut themselves off from receiving the information they need to be liberated from inner darkness.

Just as a full cup cannot hold water, these minds believe they are brimming with wisdom and knowledge, so they have no desire for further instruction. Approaching this group is tricky and must be done with care. One cannot treat them as fools, indeed they are not, yet one cannot leave them wandering in the darkness of self-importance. Perhaps, all that can be done is to show the size of the universe, the complexity of its parts, the smallness of ourselves, and the limited nature of our senses that make it hard to know anything beyond this moment.

Still another group, the saddest of them all, is those who are no longer ignorant but wish they were. These have had their minds awakened to the deeper levels of reality, but wish they could forget what they have seen so they can go back to sleep. However, the awakened mind can never return to sleep. The universe is like an endless rug glued to a floor of equal size, with the secrets of life and humanity hidden underneath. Once we pull up the rug to see what lies below, we break the adhesive holding the rug down and it can never be laid as it was again. What is learned can never be unlearned. Those who are trying to do so need to be encouraged, listened to, and shown how everyone - including themselves - would benefit if they would accept and apply what they know, rather than run from it.

The final group of people is those who are ignorant, know it, and are trying to fix it. This is the group all of us who wish to realize the best in life will be in. There is much to learn, many secrets to find, and many pieces to untangle, and then fit together. All those who escape the thicket of ignorance will forever be removing thorns. It takes a lifetime of work to find and keep wisdom and peace. If at any time we stop seeking for and applying wisdom, we will become entangled again in the briars of misunderstanding, and thus begin to suffer anew.

Just as ignorance creates more of itself like a weed that seeds your yard, so does wisdom lead to the creation of wisdom. The life that has seen the value of learning and understands the worth of knowledge, wisdom, and truth will better all they touch and themselves. Foolishness and evil, as well as virtue and wisdom, are habits that reinforce themselves. The awakened begin early to start and cultivate upward spirals, so that later they do not have to free themselves from downward ones.

All who want to be free from ignorance and the evil it creates can be, but they must first believe freedom is possible. If we see ourselves as stupid, dumb, and unable to be taught, then we will act in ways that turn our ideas into our reality. However, if we believe we can do anything, then there is no limit to what we can do. By forgetting what others have told us we are, and forsaking the ideas and limits we have accepted as a part of us, we are freed to be whatever we want.

It is my wish no one will let themselves be held in a prison made from the opinions of others, or the traditions of their culture. Everyone is capable of great things. We must climb out of the cages and find the courage to leap over our misery to the beauty and freedom on the other side. Whatever a human has done, another human can do if they apply will, wisdom, patience, courage, and focused perseverance. Let us not be content with any of our limits, especially those infringing upon the powers of our mind and the rightness of our actions.

Opening the Mind

A week had passed since Young Man had eaten the bluish berries and learned about the need for knowledge. He had begun to read the spiritual and scientific texts of his culture and thought he would discuss them with Old Beauty. After the usual hike up the mountain, he found himself at the door of her tent and at her invitation went inside.

As he looked around the candle lit area, he noticed a huge stack of books in the corner. He moved closer so he could read their names, and when he realized they were texts on science, philosophy, and religion from about every culture he could imagine, his faced furrowed and his mouth went, "Tissst". As soon as the sound finished escaping his lips, the voice of Old Beauty, smiling with sarcasm, tickled his ears, "Mastered all their wisdom already have you?" Many times before Old Beauty had demonstrated his lack of understanding, but now they were in the realm of truth. Being the son of a monk, he knew the truth. Speaking from a pose reflecting his certainty, he said, "Why do you read such nonsense, do you not know that our writings detail the straightest path to Heaven, even predicting the future, something no other book can do?"

Old Beauty took a moment to think deeply, and then replied, "Life is like an ocean, all of us are fish, and every fish eats according to its needs. Some fish are small, they stay in the shallows and though they eat little, they still eat all they need. Some fish are big, they dive into the deep and though they eat a lot, they still eat all they need. Then there is Blue the Whale, the biggest creature in the world, he dives to the bottom and opening his mouth wide consumes all he can reach. Though Blue swallows rocks, weeds, and other nasty things at times he also takes in more food than any other thing on earth. It is his food that makes him big, it is his bigness that keeps him safe, and in safety he explores the foundations of heaven and earth. Small fish, do not judge Blue for being what he is, and Blue will not judge you for being what you are."

Chapter Three

Once we realize how little we know, we have to make a choice. We can close ourselves off from the fact our understanding of reality is childlike, or we can be humbled by our smallness, and set about to become better informed about ourselves, the universe, and others.

This choice is comparable to deciding if we will sleep behind our walls, or if we will muster the courage to see what waits beyond them. If we sit in the darkness, then our mind's eye will lose the ability to see. However, if we step out from beneath the shadows of our walls, we will step into the boundless beauty and wisdom filling our world. Basking in this light, our minds will find comfort, and our eyes will discover the way to the place of peace.

Some will choose to close themselves to the treasures of the universe, choosing the familiar dark of shadow rather than the unhindered light of the real. Those who do this are like the young tree who, after seeing an ancient oak, still wanted to believe it was the biggest tree in the wood. However, those who fling themselves into the vast and beautiful unknown are like young trees whose roots dig deep, and whose branches reach high. They have seen their smallness and wish to become like the oak, able to weather the storms of life, and provide shelter for all who come to rest beneath their limbs.

Without being open, we cannot know anything about reality. This is because we are looking at all there is through the tiny hole of what we know, or what we believe we know. This is like a one who lives in a cardboard box, and watches the world go by through an acorn sized hole. There is no way they can see all the wonders and workings of the world, because their scope of vision is far too narrow.

If we only look at the world from our perspective, we are dooming ourselves and others to misunderstanding and misery. Our ignorance, due to lack of experience, poisons everything and creates decay, disorder, and death. By traveling through the different ideas, cultures, and wisdom traditions of the earth, we gradually replace our misunderstanding with understanding. Only by understanding something can one do it any good.

All we know is what we have been taught, and if we are doing all we know to do and it is not working, it is time to move on to something different. This requires a heart open to correction, guidance, and instruction. Our mind must be perpetually expanding itself into the new and unknown. Only by this type of personal exploration of reality we can gain true knowledge and accurate ideas about what reality is or is not.

Humans naturally think the ideas they have been taught are the purest expression of truth. From youth, we are told to respect and believe the counsel of family, spiritual leaders, teachers, and friends. Over time, we become accustomed to the explanations we are given, so once we are older we no longer question them. The ideas others have *about* reality have become reality for us. Thus, we sit presumptuously thinking we can accurately measure what is true and what is false by these inherited explanations of life.

This prolonged exposure to our cultural ideas not only gives us a false sense of knowing, it also enriches the ideas of our culture with a false sense of sacredness. In the end, questioning the ideas of our culture becomes the same thing as committing an evil act. This idea is a pit impossible to escape from until we realize it is not unkind to question the information others call true. It can be unkind if done in the wrong way, but a humble and kind criticism of what others assert as true is not only necessary, it is beneficial. A kind, objective, and merciless analysis of all data will not only keep us from being manipulated, it makes us and those around us deeper, wiser, and better people. It forces us to face our preconceptions, see our illusions, and to cultivate our minds.

Humans generally get angry when you question what they tell you is true, because what they are saying is a part of their world view. If you question their view of the world, then you are casting doubt upon the ideas they have based their entire life upon. This is why thinking outside of the box is usually frowned upon no matter the box it is you are in.

Nevertheless, if we do not question what we are told, we are inviting into our life an endless string of problems. Those who taught you were taught by others, who were taught by others, who were taught by still others. Most systems only teach those within them ideas they accept as true. Rarely, if ever, does any system teach its students to critically analyze the ideas they are being taught by its representatives. As ideas move from person to person, and away from the times in which they were debated, eventually they become standards by which one measures the virtue of any given action. They become the basis of thought, or a social norm.

However, what happens if false ideas and errant beliefs make their way into this cycle at an early point? Then entire religions, sciences, philosophies, and styles of government end up being built upon poor logic, false information, and traditional illusions. This is why in earlier times most everyone believed the earth was flat, you could drain blood to cure diseases, and the moon was the reason people went crazy.

We have to examine everything we have ever been told. If we do not, we will find ourselves living in a world built from the ideas of another that may or may not be right. This is how people end up doing stupid actions in the name of wisdom, hating in the name of love, and murdering in the name of life. This must stop and only wisdom can end it.

All of us are open to some form of input and advice. We have trusted gurus, wise friends, old preachers, a loving family member, or some other source we will accept new ideas and correction from. However, even the wisest can err and the most loving can be misled or misleading. We each must search widely and broadly every nook of heaven, earth, and ourselves for truth, lest we end up becoming the pawns or victims of false information.

Our sense of right and wrong, our dreams, even who we are, is created by the culture we are born into. Since this is the case, it is perfectly possible what we have been taught to believe is *right* is really *wrong,* and what we have been taught to believe is *wrong* is really *right.* Suicide bombers and Christian Crusaders took the lives of innocent people for the furtherance of truth and peace. They thought they were doing what was best, because of the definitions of right and wrong given to them by their trusted teachers. Governments also spin the truth and instill erroneous ideas in order to control their people: North Korea, Catholic Europe, Nazi Germany, and Communist Russia are a few examples of this. Information does not have to be true in order to influence someone they just have to believe it is.

If the majority of the world were Muslim, then any Hindu ideas would be wrong, and if the majority of the world were Hindu, then Islamic ideas would be seen as wrong. The system of understanding that fills your mind gives you the standards by which *right* and *wrong* are judged. This is why we must go deeper than any existing system and higher than any known authority in order to find out what right and wrong really are. Our understanding on these topics cannot be defined by some cherished book, the tales of the ancestors, or the equations of some noted researcher. They must be based upon deep and objective study of the external world and *all* it contains. Just as we cannot plant one apple tree and profess to be master gardeners in possession of an orchard, so we cannot study one book and then profess to be sages or saints filled with indisputable knowledge of ultimate truth.

All of us are members of one race. Yet, we come from different places where we were taught different things about ourselves and our world. All of us have room to grow in our understanding. If we can grasp these things, then we are empowered to understand, honor, and learn from each other. If we could all realize this unity, we could unlock mysteries and experience beauties we have never seen. More wonderful than both of these, is the fact for the first time everyone on earth might live in harmony.

All things in the entire universe, including humanity, are in a constant state of change; nothing in all of reality is as it was yesterday. When we try to remain the same we are attempting the impossible. If trees do not grow they die, if water does not flow it stagnates, and if people do not daily increase in understanding their information rots and eventually becomes poison.

All living things in existence are always giving to, and receiving from, the world around them. If at any point this exchange stops, the living thing grows ill, and if uncured will die. Plants cannot live without continually taking from and giving to the environment. Even though they exist as individual entities, plants must be in complete cooperation with the world around them in order to maintain life. The same is true for animals. They must always be taking in and giving out for life to be healthy and continue. If the inflow stops, the creature uses all its resources, withers and dies. If the outflow stops, then the wastes left over from what it has eaten will become toxic and the toxicity, if uncorrected, will extinguish the life.

Humans are a part of the natural world and function in the same way, though most of us like to think we are above nature. We picture ourselves as superior creatures, and act as though we are somehow apart from the world around us. We mistreat and abuse the things and people we contact, and then wonder why we are suffering. People too must comply with the principle of openness and sharing that guides all other living things. If we take and never replenish, we will kill others. If we give and never take, we will kill ourselves.

Humanity's mental world is just as complex as the physical world, and we can understand the mental by comparing it to the material. If in our minds we do not take in the air of exploration, the water of wisdom, the light of compassion, and the food of respect we will die inside. This inner death kills what is around us by degrees. Likewise, if we do not give these things to the people we meet, we are starving them, and eventually they too will die inside and we will be to blame.

If we isolate ourselves from the rest of our race and the world, there will never be peace, and like a body cut into pieces the whole will die. Openness is the key to the door of personal and worldwide betterment, harmony, and understanding. If we do not open our minds, and lose our pride, our world will forever be filled with war and misunderstanding. If this happens, there will be no one to blame but ourselves.

Openness does not mean I have to agree with everything someone else says. Do roses grow in the same way as lilies, or do the redwoods climb like vines? In nature, things do not share the same particulars, but they share many generalities. Nature does not force them into conformity, but allows them to be what they are, and to do what they must in order to fulfill their individual needs.

Openness works in the same way. To be open means to have respect for all recorded human wisdom, and to explore it with the goal of gaining a more accurate understanding of reality by fair, honest, and non-biased research. The goal is not to make others more like us, nor is it to remain just as we are, it is to bring all of us into harmony with each other and the principles of wisdom.

Open books are the only ones that can teach us. Open windows are the only ones that light can pour through. Open eyes are the only ones who receive the beauty of sight, and open hearts the only ones who receive the gift of love. We cannot afford to close ourselves off from all the forms of wisdom filling the earth. Understanding each other and our world is the only thing that can banish the ignorance leading to evil, and teach the good that will provide for us a future.

Beyond Fear

The day was dark, and the sky screamed lighting moments before crying thunder. Young Man became worried about Old Beauty and made his way through the storm up to her tent. Upon arriving, he found Old Beauty face down. Fearing she had been struck by lightning he ran to her, but just as he began to shake her, a swift and surprising powerful blow knocked him into the corner. "What on earth do you think you are doing?" she quipped. Young Man replied, "I feared you were dead but obviously you are not." Old Beauty burst out, "Dead! I may not be young but I am far from dead. I was sleeping." "Sleeping", Young Man replied, "Aren't you afraid to sleep in a storm like this?" Old Beauty smiled with appreciation at Young Man's concern and replied, "Fear is a waste of life".

After handing Young Man a towel to dry with she began, "Once a very mean man caught a very beautiful lady, blindfolded her, and took her to an unknown desert island a little ways from the mainland. Before leaving her there, he said, 'Beneath the waves are zombies that will eat your legs if you try to swim away. Wait here till I return.' The beautiful lady loved her beautiful legs and did not want them to be eaten, frantically she nodded in agreement and the mean man went away."

"Day after day this happened until she was old and near death. No longer were her legs beautiful and she had been there so long she did not care if they were eaten if it meant she could be free. Jumping into the water she found, much to her surprise, not only were there no zombies, but the way was so shallow she could walk on the ocean floor. If only she had looked under the waves she could have become free. Even if there had been zombies she could have watched their movements, studied their natures, and found a way to best them but now her life was gone. Her vivid imaginings and deep desire to preserve live had robbed her of life. Now, the freedom she could have lived in, she will experience only long enough to die."

Chapter Four

Having seen the need to deepen our understanding and open our hearts, we must learn to move beyond our fears. We cannot be open unless we are fearless, and we are not truly fearless unless we have opened ourselves to experience and knowledge. Openness without fearlessness can see the truth, but does not accept or conform to it. Fearlessness without openness becomes unbalanced, stubborn, and arrogant.

Fear is a state of mind we enter when we perceive something bad is happening or will happen to us, things we enjoy, or others we care about. This state of mind can range from very mild to extreme, depending on the amount of discomfort we expect to be caused, the amount of distaste we already have for what we expect, and the amount of loss we believe it will cause.

The harmful element can be anything real or imagined we find scary to look at, scary to think about, or scary to experience. It can be as simple as the neighbor's dog chasing us every time we leave our home, or as complex as the idea that we are going to be rejected by those who taught us life's meaning.

Whatever is going to cause us pain, loss, or change, we usually make into a bad thing, and then experience a strong negative emotion whenever we see or imagine the bad thing coming to pass. This is a very basic and important event that happens in every human mind, so we might avoid harm. The negative feeling that comes is meant to cause us to do whatever it takes to remain beyond the reach of the harmful elements in our world.

The problem is our minds do not come with a built in fear detector. There is no device in the brain behaving like a metal detector, distinguishing real threats from imaginary ones. Thus, fearful emotions can be triggered by things that are harmless, or even beneficial. Fear is as much a product of social conditioning, and personal belief, as it is a product of real danger.

Not only does our fear detector fail at telling us what we should and should not fear, it cannot tell the difference between things existing in the real world, and things existing only in our imagination. Many are bound by unreal fears when they could be free, if only they would measure their thoughts by fact and not feelings, by logic and not social norm.

If our minds do not detect what we really should be afraid of naturally, and cannot tell the difference between real threats and imagined ones, where do all these fears come from? They come to us through the ones we love and trust: our friends, families, spiritual guides, and teachers. From childhood we are taught what we should fear, and what we should not.

Some give their children racial fears - teaching them certain groups of people are vile and should be avoided or hated. Some give their children supernatural fears - teaching them there are beings roaming the night that have to be made happy or kept away by offering, obedience, or magic. Others put social fears into their young - making them afraid of being seen by others as low class, out of style, evil, or unwanted. Still others pump material fears into youthful minds - telling them poverty is the same as divine disapproval, or wealth can only be obtained by evil means. In truth, there is usually a fear filled brew made up of all this and more that is poured into the minds of every person from the time they are born till the day they die.

Every culture and subculture comes complete with their own ideas of what is good or bad, and from this indoctrination fear arises. If our culture says turnips are good, then a lack of turnips must be bad, a fact that causes the mind to fear a turnip-less state. If our culture says blue eyes are honorable and having brown eyes are a reason for shame, parents will be filled with anxiety over their child's eye color. These are just two examples, but the list of culturally instilled fears is almost endless, and changes as the standards of the culture implanting them change.

In this way, fear is created within a group and once created it keeps itself alive because those in the group pump their fears into everyone they have a relationship with. The deeper the relationship, the more deeply instilled the fears become. People are thereby filled with fear and in turn pass them onto those they have relationships with. Thus, cowardice spreads like a weed; the fears of the forebears infesting and troubling their offspring for generations on end.

Most of us are living our lives according to the rules and fears of people who have died long ago, because we do not question and objectively analyze the things society tells us. We accept the answers about life given to us and do not seek the true nature of reality. Thus, we sit in ignorance thinking we have knowledge fearful of illusions. This demonstrates why in order to be open we must be fearless, and why in order to be fearless we must cure our lack of understanding.

We must strike fear from our lives. It is okay to be afraid and worry. All of us have things that send shivers down our spine, or cause our heart to skip a beat. The answer is to change the way we relate to fear. Rather than it being a fence we cannot cross, or a beast we must avoid, we need to make it a teacher. Fear viewed in this way instructs us, it allows us to examine its advice, and then to accept or move beyond it based on whether or not it is rooted in reason, grounded in reality, reflects possibility, and expresses wisdom. Only when fear is viewed like this can we free ourselves from the prejudice, superstitions, and cultural taboos that prevent us from experiencing freedom and joy.

If we do not change the way we relate to fear, our minds will be trapped in a prison even though our bodies move about freely. Fear numbs the mind, enslaves the will, and weakens reason, so one feels they are jammed into a box even though they sit in a forest. Fear is not useless, but if we misunderstand and fail to question it, we will find ourselves locked into doing a great many useless things.

The goal of every human should not be merely having the courage to face fear, but to maintain a state of mind where fear plays no role in the decision making process. Do not let yourself be intimidated by rank because no one on earth is better or worse than you. Neither let yourself be fearful of creatures or events, because we have minds capable of adapting to all things with haste and dominance. Above all, do not fear what cannot be changed or fret over what cannot be controlled. If you do this, you will never have peace because you will forever be trying to live up to unrealistic expectations.

Work, hunger, change, decay, loss of material possessions, and death cannot be avoided. These are natural processes that have been active in our world as far back as human records go, if not from the beginning. Everything new grows old, all that feeds hungers, and all that is born dies. We can either make peace with what we cannot change or let our anxieties ruin what is and all that could be. Fear is a thief that steals joy, beauty, and peace from us. However, those who seek and apply wisdom can control and conquer their fears, thereby taking back the gems of life it robbed.

We cannot afford to let others determine who we are, what we do, and what we can become. Yet, this is exactly what fear causes us to do if we leave it unchecked. Can you imagine how our world would be if our forefathers had allowed fears and social norms to rule their thoughts and actions? Think of all the people who have dared to think differently in times when the price to do so was death. Think of the adventurers who plunged into the unknown, and brought back countless treasures and ideas that have bettered human life. Think of the fearless warriors whose actions protected emperors, created empires, and gave birth to freedom. Now, imagine what the world would be like if all these had not broken the bonds of fear? Fearlessness, when coupled with wisdom, is the beginning of greatness. Let us all then become great.

Fear causes the mind to imprison itself behind the bars of its own imagination. It is like someone who has been held prisoner all their life by a three foot tall fence. They dare not jump over it merely because they have been told all their life they should not or cannot do so. As long as we lack the courage to objectively study and see if the things we have been told match reality, we will forever be filled with the guilt of another, robbed of our strength, and cut off from truth. As long as we allow fear of what others may think about us or do to us to control our actions, we are their puppets. Their desires - no matter how sincere they may be - become the strings determining our every thought and action.

It does not matter if everyone wants to hug or hit me; I was not born to make them happy, and they were not born to make me happy. Each of us are commanders of our own vessel and no other human, even those who profess to speak on behalf of Heaven, have the right to dictate to us what we should think or do, as long as we are not infringing upon the rights of another. If we are not brave, the thoughts, words, opinions, rewards, and punishments of the outside world will shape our unique and priceless life into a cog for their machine.

Even if everyone in the world heaps shame upon us, it does not mean we have done or thought something we ought to be ashamed of. True shame does not come from failing to live up to a standard held by someone else, it comes from within and rises from a personal realization of truth. Therefore, we should not fear the guilt mortals try to heap upon us when we trash useless customs and challenge treasured traditions. What we should be wary of is violating the principles of life, and the freedoms the universe gives to all who dwell within her.

We have within us pure potential, and how we choose to shape ourselves, or allow something besides ourselves to shape us, determines what we shall become. Jesus and Judas had the same human nature, as did Hitler and Buddha. We can enlighten ourselves and others, or we can cast both into an impenetrable darkness. All we are or will become rests soundly upon how we use our wills, our minds, and our bodies. The only future is the one our choices build from this moment. Fate is an illusion those who are too indoctrinated, too fearful, or too weak to think and choose take comfort in. Let us then stop admiring others, destroy our idols and limits, and train body and mind until we have turned our aspirations into reality.

We should not fear injury, because to spend one's life in fear is more harmful. How many will not stand up to bullies, abusive spouses, or harsh dictators because they fear what might happen? I challenge all who are suffering to look at what is happening, and ask if the cost of freedom would be any greater than the price they are already paying. Pain is an unavoidable part of living, but we can choose how and why we hurt. Some hurt because ticks and leeches are draining their life away, and some hurt because they are pulling the parasites out of their mind and life. It is wiser to hurt in order to obtain freedom, than it is to allow internal and external parasites to daily drain you of your life. Those who strive for freedom find peace in the end, while those who allow parasites to rule suffer endlessly.

It is not until we let go of the old familiar fears that we can find joy and freedom. We cannot find anything new until we become dissatisfied with what we already have. We cannot soar until we cut away all the illusionary beliefs and thoughtless habits we have allowed to infest our mind. Fear is like a lion on a chain, it harms only those who do not move beyond its reach.

We use our strength to build the dream of another, exchange our life for materials, and then use those materials as fuel to keep this cycle going. We are all slaves to a beastly system we created, but freedom is attainable for all who will move beyond the things they know into the deep and unfamiliar waters of the unknown. Our minds may fill with anxiety as we step away from the safety of home into the unlit wilderness of the unknown, but without this step we would forever remain in our current state. Fear not the change, but rather the consequences of remaining the same.

Closed minded and fearful people love their ideas, and the comfort they find in them. They protect them violently and refuse to accept any reality or truth that does not match what they already think. People like this have forgotten, or have never received the lessons taught by the natural world. The only things that do not grow are either dead or dying. We are constantly improving our thoughts and actions, or we are slipping into a quiet decay that will corrupt every part of our life.

Those who fear the deep will remain in the shallows forever, and there they will endlessly be tossed by the waves of life. However, those who make the deep their home will dwell in stillness and peace; the submarine is not even slightly shaken by the wind bashing the boat to bits.

Fear prevents us from discovering what it means to live, and taints the brightest moments of our life with anxieties about an uncertain future and a certain death. Those who accept their mortality, and make peace with death are empowered to live a life of strength, boldness, and freedom. Those who fear, hasten their own demise by the very habits of thought and action they have created to forget all things are daily moving closer to their demise.

We cannot find fulfillment, much less happiness, as long as we live out our deepest dreams and desires through the achievements, fictions, and systems of others. Nothing is a substitute for personal achievement. One who writes the story of their lives in the ink of personal accomplishment will find it better than a house filled with the joys of others.

By accepting endlessness as our boundary and nothingness as our cage we can realize the potentials within us and achieve freedom. Once we do this, the universe and all it contains becomes our teacher. Freely and without guilt our minds can access all the wisdom and truth there is, without concern for such trifling things as who said it and what type of words they used. Having done this, nothing can control us, only infinity can contain us, and our only enemy becomes the evils and illusions we have within ourselves. Only after we have escaped all unreal systems of thought and action can we escape the final fear - the fear of losing control.

The illusion of control is at the root of many human fears, and is reinforced as long as we keep our minds closed to the bigger picture. We think we possess something, thus we fear it being taken away. We think we can control circumstances, thus we fear failure. Control and ownership are complete illusions wounding our mind and filling us with unnecessary grief.

The material things we think we own are just a bunch of wood, minerals, and synthetic substances that will eventually become useless and forgotten. Those who acquire vast possessions not only lose peace, but quickly become the property of the things they own. They fear their treasures will break or be taken from them. They toil slavishly to preserve, acquire, or replace the material objects they love and measure accomplishment by.

The ideas we think of as ours are not our exclusive property. The wisdom, truth, understanding, and knowledge any of us possess, or at least think we possess, is mostly made up from the realizations others have had. Where then is room for intellectual pride since every mental commodity was given to us, or grew from the seed another planted? At times we may gain new and unique insights, or discover unknown truths, but these are like fruits picked from atop a borrowed ladder.

We can understand this better by comparing it to the way sculptors craft new forms from old stone. Did the sculptor create their own consciousness? No, it was created without their consent by parents, and kept alive by a brain smarter than the mind it produces. How about the skills needed to shape the stone? Did the sculptor merely wake up one day with the methods and understanding needed to create a masterpiece? No, their entire life was shaped by the environment, information, and people surrounding them.

What of the tools used by the sculptor? These were brought into being by the hand of a metal smith, the ax of a lumber jack, and the guts of a mountain. Even if the sculptor did put the tools together, they did not make the tree, the iron, or the stone. Anything accomplished by humans does not happen independently. Billions of other people and things, working together with our circumstances and will, bring them to pass. If we try to take complete credit for any of our achievements, it merely shows we have no idea about the size, interdependence, or flow of reality.

Outcomes too are beyond our control. We exist in a universe ruled by immense forces we still do not completely understand and cannot manipulate. Not only is the universe beyond our will, but we share it with billions of other beings, each having a will that is as far beyond our control as the motions of the sun. We must plan, learn, and attempt, but the outcome is not only a matter of effort, it is also determined by time, place, circumstance, and chance.

The only control we can ever have is over our own will. Beauty moves to ugliness, power turns to weakness, and what we own becomes the property of another. Even our mind is only ours for a little while. In the end, it is taken by yet another uncontrollable power - the power of death.

This is not depressing, it is the way things are, and the ultimate reason why we should seek and obtain freedom from fear. Through fearlessness we realize the power and liberty of the will. With this realization comes the ability to harness this power. Once we possess this ability we can share it with others, thus fearlessness liberates not only ourselves, but all who will heed our words and follow our example. By losing the illusion of control, and harmonizing with the powers guiding the universe, we can acquire the ultimate treasures: happiness, truth, and peace.

All we have is made from the mental materials left behind by those who lived before us, and what we leave behind will become materials future generations use to build their lives. Thus, we should strive to leave foundations like mountains and treasures like desert wells, so they can know how to craft themselves and treat their world. Freedom of mind is the sturdiest stone, and fearlessness the sweetest of springs.

How Words and Symbols Blind Us

One day, Young Man was in the city, and saw two groups of priests arguing over a segment of religious text. He drew closer, and as he listened realized the two groups were saying the exact same thing using different words. Seeking to bring some resolution to the situation, he spoke up and pointed out the substance of what they were saying was the same they were only using different titles to describe it. While his words did succeed in bringing unity, it was not the type he intended to create. Rather than admitting they were both speaking of the same thing, they both turned on him and begin to express how foolish he was and how little he understood about the holy writings. Perplexed and let down, Young Man decided to go to Old Beauty and relate to her his experience; she always seemed to find a way to sooth his pain.

He made his way up the Mountain's path as usual, and after taking a seat beside the fire where Old Beauty was readying some tea, told her the story. A smile crossed her face and she exclaimed, "So you have been learning something, I thought you were deaf!" Though these words might seem harsh, her manner of speaking, and the joy with which she said it, caused Young Man to chuckle and his care eased a bit. Just then the tea began to whistle, and after pouring each of them a cup, Old Beauty made her way to a box on the shelf, and pulled out some strange looking coins. Laying them in front of him, she explained these were from a place called America. After relating how they worked, she began to teach.

Old Beauty said, "You have in front of you ten quarters, ten dimes, and ten nickels. Let us pretend you owe me seventy-six cents. Using only the coins in front of you, I need you to pay me." Young Man thought for a moment and after some hesitation said, "I may be missing some deeper possibility, but I cannot give you seventy-six cents using only these coins, the sliver ones can only be added together to create payments in multiples of five." After scowling for a moment to pretend he had got it wrong, Old Beauty's face softened into a smile and she said, "You are absolutely right!"

Old Beauty then reached into her pocket and pulled out a penny, "It seems an insignificant little thing does it not, yet without it you cannot pay or collect in precise amounts. This is how it is with set systems. People who are devoted to any unvarying and strict system become unable to produce responses exactly reflecting reality. They can come close, even to within one cent, but they cannot be precise. This lack of precision adds up over time, and in the end the sum of all their ideas and understanding differs greatly from the real. When two people from two concrete systems try to speak, it is a like a man behind a window of blue glass arguing about the color of the sun with a man seated behind a pane of green."

Chapter Five

Now that our ignorance is known, our minds are open, and our wills filled with courage let us pull the mask of words from the face of reality.

Symbols are at the center of all human civilizations, past or present, and preserve the events and codes of those civilizations long after they're gone. The most common use of symbols is to express what we have in our minds to another, and this expression we call language. Language can take the form of pictures, figures, or sounds and without it the workings of our world would slow to a halt, if not stop altogether. It is for this reason each of us are taught the symbols of our culture from the day we are born, and after we have learned them they are used to teach us everything we know.

So common is the use of symbols most of us have forgotten that the words, pictures, and figures we use to express ourselves are symbols at all. Yet, if we are going to accurately understand anything, we must consider deeply the symbols we use to express ourselves until we grasp what they are, how they are used, and how they are understood by others. The person who fails to analyze and grasp the nature of symbols, especially words - spoken or written - will never understand the truth.

Before anything can be discussed it must first be understood and defined correctly. Let us begin by asking, 'What are words?' I am focusing on words, because they are the most common tool we use to let others know what we are thinking. However, I would have the reader keep in mind what is true of words applies to all other motions, symbols, signs, or pictures used to convey any meaning whatsoever.

Words are little boats carrying the information from our minds into the minds of others in a way they can understand. This is true whether they are written, spoken, or signed. Words are like the labels on cereal boxes, and their meaning is like the cereal. Those who see the image know what substance the box contains, and so know how or how not to use them.

Words do not exist by themselves they are small parts in the machine of society. Words let the people within a community understand where they need to go, how to get there, how the world works, and the reason they have for doing what they do.

Where do words come from? As we noted above they are parts of a specific community, and it is that community which creates them, gives them meaning, and then teaches them to others. This leads us to the first important discovery about words - they do not all come from a single 'Word Factory'. There is not a massive building somewhere every human goes to in order to receive the language they will use to express themselves. Neither is there a dictionary in the sky giving absolute and unchanging meaning to words.

The reader can get a better understanding of what this means by comparing it to the metric system of measurement. The metric system is a common mathematical language used all around the world, so a Russian can understand the measurements taken by a scientist in Korea. This mathematical language is understood by people on different sides of the earth, because the symbols are given the same meaning no matter where, or whom, the teacher is. Words are not like this, they vary greatly from place to place and person to person, they change with time, and often have more than one meaning.

Every set of words, called a language, is unique to the people and place it comes from, and any who enter from the outside easily and often misunderstand. This makes it difficult to speak with or understand correctly someone from another culture.

Even when a person learns the language of another group, this does not mean they can fully understand or express themselves to those people. This is because even though a common word system is used by a nation, such as America's use of English, the same word can have different meanings depending on where you are within that nation, and who it is you are speaking to.

For example, I am from Kentucky, and I call the knitted wool cap that keeps your head warm in winter a *boggin*. Once, I was going to school in Northern California during February, and preparing to face the early morning chill, I asked my friend if he had seen my *boggin*. An expression crossed his face showing me he had no idea what I was talking about, and he replied, "A what?" After I had described it to him he said, "Oh, you mean a beanie!" Instantly, in my mind I got a picture of a man wearing a silly hat with a propeller on top and I said, "No, not a beanie, this cap is made of wool, doesn't have a propeller, and keeps the heat from leaving my head". Finally he realized what I was talking about, and donning my wooly head dress I finally got to start my day. We could not communicate with each other, because we were using different words - different symbols - to describe the same thing. Communication did not take place until we talked about the hat's nature and appearance, instead of what we call it.

Having seen how words can confuse the simple act of finding a piece of head gear, you can imagine how topics such as the existence of God and what truth is can become a hopeless maze.

Not only does each of us have our own idea about what words mean, but the ideas we have been taught with those words are tainted by the opinions and goals of the people teaching them. This is why someone who does not make the effort to look beyond words will never be able to truly understand themselves or others; much less the universe we live in.

If you do not learn to look at the meaning rather than the words conveying it, you will be confused no matter what else you do. Each of us must learn to look at the thing being talked about rather than the words used to describe it if we are going to truly know anything. If we let ourselves get stuck on the words, we will be arguing about concepts and names, and in the end get nothing but frustrated.

Words, symbols, names, titles, all these are just stickers placed by humanity on everything in existence. No entity, object, idea, or energy in the universe comes with a label on it telling us its name. *Tree, dog, cat, right, wrong, good, bad* and all other words are merely labels we have created so we can communicate to one another. Everything you can see right now, even yourself, has been given its name by humanity. I am not what I am called, and neither is anything else, these are only titles others can use to refer to me.

Among the most vital lessons we can learn is the habit of describing things based on their substance and not their name tag. What I call a *tree* you may call an *eert*, however the object we are talking about is exactly the same. By walking over to that object, touching the bark, measuring the height, watching how it comes about, grows, and dies, we can communicate to each other what it is we are talking about.

As with trees, so with all objects whether they exist only within us, mental, whether we can all sense and interact with them, eternal. For example, what group A calls *love* group B may call *velt*. This seems harmless enough, and it is as long as they are talking to a group of people who understand the words they are using. However, if the leaders of group A meet with group B and find the root of their culture is *velt* and not *love,* they may think those in group B are barbarians. From this wrong idea may flow fear, and from fear pours a countless number of poor decisions and horrible acts. This is why we must study deeply into the words, cultures, and beliefs of others so we do not mistake those who are allies as enemies.

If we do not take the time to look beyond words, we will find we are viewing all things in the universe through a fog of misunderstanding. Just as a person who looks at a can of *peaches* labeled *apples* will never know what the can really contains, those who mistake concepts and words for reality will never find what is real.

Misnaming of anything in reality is extremely easy to do since limited and error prone humans have named everything. We can understand this when we look at how children are named. There are different people who are called by the same name and individuals who are known by different names to different people. As it is with people, so it is with all other things in existence.

All too often we never see what is really happening, because we shrink what we see, usually without even realizing we are doing so, into our current understanding. We define and understand our universe according to what it is called, and what we have been told, when we should define it based on what it is, and how it works.

This error is multiplied by the fact that when we do not know what something is, we name it according to what we *think* it is, rather than admitting ignorance and taking time to learn. It is like seeing a potbellied pig for the first time, and instead of taking the time to find out what it is, we call it a warthog because it has some of the same parts. Then, once we have called it a warthog our mind starts to recall all the horrible stories we have heard about how mean they are. This in turn causes us to either frantically run away from a perfectly harmless creature or try to kill it, all of this because we did not take the time to learn the creature's true nature. In this way, we often misname all that is unknown to us, and in turn behave incorrectly in regards to it.

We call things that are good and holy evil and vile, because they are unfamiliar and strange to us. Many wonderful things are forsaken and many wonderful people killed, because someone did not take the time to find out what they actually were.

It is easier to call the unknown *evil* and the unfamiliar *bad*. Then, we do not have to worry about being wrong, seeing our faults, or concern ourselves with the changes such realizations would require. However, it is much more rewarding to search into the nature of all things, because then we can live based upon the way things really are and not according to the way we have been taught. In this way, we build our lives and futures upon the substance of reality, and not just upon other people's descriptions and opinions of it. We build upon truth rather than illusion, and we live in the real rather than in our concepts of reality.

Words give us our understanding of reality, our understanding of reality guides our choices, our choices make us what we are, and what we are determines the quality of our lives. By naming things incorrectly, we can ruin our lives.

A good illustration of this is found in the cockpit of an airplane. Pilots determine where they are, and how to get where they are going, based upon tools giving them their location in relation to true north. If they fly for hours, and are just one degree off course they can end up hundreds of miles away from their destination with no place to land. It would be like trying to fly from California to Indiana and ending up over the Gulf of Mexico.

The same is true in life. If we call things *great* that are only *okay,* at the end of our lives we will have accomplished very trivial things believing to have done something great. Words matter because we interpret their meanings as being accurate descriptions of reality, and if we use wrong words then we make a wrong reality.

There are people who call pure things evil and evil things pure. They end up destroying their own lives, and since no one lives in isolation, those they come into contact with as well. I think about all the dogmatic people, religious and secular, who go about life hating, judging, belittling, and hurting others while calling what they are doing teaching, bettering, and helping. I also think about suicide bombers and brainwashed warriors who kill innocent people thinking they are defending people, furthering love, or bettering the world.

We must take apart every word, idea, and concept entering our life, in order to make sure we are not hating in the name of love or hurting in the name of healing. We must look at meanings behind the words and not the words themselves. This is why we must be fearless. We have to not be afraid to question the words of everyone no matter what their rank or relationship to us. Neither can we fear the loss of their favor or the consequences of our honest objections.

It does not matter who is speaking to us be they rich or poor, free or slave, king or beggar, we need to respectively, calmly, and peacefully look beyond their words into the substance of what they are saying. If we do this, we will see the foolishness of people we once thought wise, the compassion of people we once thought savage, and the beauty of things we once despised as evil.

Many also fail to understand the labels and words we use to explain the world change over time. What the word *cool* meant one hundred years ago is different than what it can mean today. It was once a reference to temperature, but now it has grown to be an expression of how we feel about something.

We cannot measure the expressions and ideas of the past by putting our meanings onto the words they used or measuring their understanding by our own. Those who insist upon doing so will only become confused and confuse others. Imagine calling everyone you think of as being happy *gay* or explaining to your otherwise smart friend how their new fireplace is absolutely not *cool* because of the heat coming out of it.

Words are necessary things, they allow us to express what is in our minds to each other, and help us to understand the universe we live in. However, if we do not understand they are just stickers we have put on the world differing from culture to culture, place to place, and person to person that change over time, all the good they could have done will be turned into harm. Never forget our words are not at all the things we are describing, and our perceptions of reality are not reality.

In terms of direction there is no east, west, north, or south, these are all just titles we have given to the directions we can move from our current location. All of space and time is one complete whole that cannot be divided, even though it is filled with many things.

There is no *Far East*, *West*, or *Middle East* in terms of human society. The different governments of earth have drawn lines upon the ground, and upon the minds of those who live within those boundaries. However, like the symbols and directions we use these are just human conventions. There is no actual division between the peoples of the earth; only those we have made real by our collective belief in them. We are one family residing in the house called earth.

African, European, Asian, Jew, Indian, Native American, Mexican, Russian, Greek, and all the other people we have named for their unlikeness to us are not really different at all. There is only one race of people dwelling on the face of the earth, and that is the human race. As long as we filter reality through the words helping us understand it, we can never realize the common humanity and reality we all share.

The words we use divide us from ourselves, our world, and from one another. This disunity, unless remedied, will eventually destroy us. In war, generals know if they can divide a kingdom they can destroy it. As long as people do not see mind and body as one they will never be well. As long as we fail to understand how our every action impacts everything and everyone on the earth, we have no future. Our actions have no end to their influence once they have been committed. As long as we insist upon seeing ourselves, and those from our own culture, as different from those of other cultures we cannot understand the sufferings, beliefs, or needs of our fellow man.

Whenever someone says *us* they instantly create a group called *them*. Whenever one says *this* they create *that*. The symbolic systems, verbal and written, we use to understand reality are limited in their usefulness and by their very nature separate and divide. When we say *apples*, we have made it clear we are not referring to any other object. When we have said *love*, we have made it clear we are not referring to hate. If words did not specify, then communication would be impossible. At the same time, we must understand the limited capacity of words, otherwise communication will be filled with error and generate harm we never intended.

Words are reflections of meaning, meaning arises from the mind as it reacts to the things it senses, and sense is but a foggy reflection of the material world around us. In the end, all communication is incomplete and fuzzy like a radio signal cutting in and out due to poor reception. For this reason, we must communicate with one another deeply, and be knowledgeable about the limits built into anything intended to convey meaning.

Those who pretend these limits do not exist, those who name things according to their appearance and not their substance, divide things that ought to be joined, join things that ought to be divided, desire things that do not matter, and make undesirable things that are important. Such behavior can only produce confusion, and in proportion to the confusion in the world, there is an equal amount of suffering.

Those who get beyond words no longer passively look at the world or lazily accept the things they are told. Forced to think deeply as they strive to name things according to their nature, they slowly begin to see reality as it really is. The amount of happiness one has is in proportion to the amount of illusions they have cast out of their thoughts.

There is no amount of words that can accurately describe all the depth and wonder existing within and beyond our universe. Yet, we can experience this wonder, and have within ourselves a truth and peace that expression only corrupts. However, this experience cannot be had if we lock ourselves away in cages of ignorance, narrowness, and fear. Neither can it be had if we hold to systems of expression that obscure as much as they reveal.

When we sweep away all the artificial divisions of body, mind, people, and place we suddenly find ourselves in a limitless moment. Gazing into the boundless moment, we see the unity of all things and the oneness of the entire human race.

As long as we view ourselves as separate or somehow different from each other, we cannot have or give true compassion. As long as we see ourselves as separate from our universe, we cannot see the need for right action or know our place in it. As long as we divide the body and mind, we will never know what it means to be whole.

Right Calculations

One day, Young Man decided to climb down one side of the Mountain to a valley he had never explored. He gauged his distance, wove his rope, made his hike, and repelled down the side of the cliff only to realize he had cut his rope fifty feet too short. He looked around to see if he could make it down some other way, but he could not and saddened climbed back to the top of the Mountain.

With a frown upon his face, he walked heavily into the tent where Old Beauty sat. When she asked what was wrong, he told her and she began to speak, "One sunny spring day a hive of bees that had slept through the winter began to venture out into the forests and fields around their hive to gather honey for the winter to come. They knew the winter was going to be harsh, so they threw themselves into the work, so they might rest and be safe through the coming cold."

"The whole hive was bustling with diligent little bees, each being masters at their own task. Some bees were craftsmen, some bees were collectors, some served the queen, and some protected the hive. However, there was one set of bees that had the most sacred job of all; they were the mathematicians in charge of telling the bees much how nectar they needed to collect for the winter to survive. They studied day and night to ensure they were without flaw, and related to the hive what it needed to do to live."

"The year passed, winter came, and when the summer sun rose on the sleepy little hive, it found no one was sleeping because they were all dead. The mathematicians had erred, and since everyone had assumed them correct they all died. Do not let anyone do your math for you, and never quit until your calculations are as certain as the rising of the sun."

Chapter Six

Right calculations are made up of two parts: right measurements and right equations. To have right measurements means to have correct data about what ever subject, idea, or thing is being talked about. Right equations means having a system of understanding that properly uses the data we put in to produce correct answers. I know this is a spacey concept, so we will use a simple mathematical illustration to help explain.

We all remember two plus two equals four from school. This simple equation provides for us all we need to grasp the above concepts. The numbers two and two are the measurements or data, and the equation $A+B=C$ is the system we are using to get our answer, four.

Let us imagine a driver who mistakenly thinks the two gallons of gas in their car will give them twenty-five miles of travel per gallon. Adding twenty-five to twenty-five they discover they have enough gas to make a fifty mile trip. They only need to travel forty-five miles altogether, so even though their gas gauge is broken, and they know they'll be cutting it close, they confidently jump in and set about their business.

All is going well until on the way back home their engine suddenly dies, and they are stuck on the freeway. Their car only gets seventeen miles to the gallon, and now they have to wait hours in the hot sun until help arrives. Was their equation, $A+B=C$, wrong? No, the system they used was correct, but the data they put into it led them to an incorrect conclusion causing them to suffer.

Now, let us consider what will happen if their data is right, but the system they use to make their answers - their equation - is wrong. Time has passed and the above car owner needs to make another trip, but this time their destination is only eight miles away. Their gas gauge is still broken, so they still have to figure out if there is enough gas in their tank to make the trip. The person learned their lesson last time and knows their car only gets seventeen miles per gallon. However, due to the amount of time they spent in the sun a few days ago, they are not thinking straight, and so they use an incorrect equation.

The driver has the right distance their car can travel on a gallon of gas, seventeen miles, but instead of using A+B=C, they turn their addition symbol on its side making A x B=C. Then they do the math, eight multiplied by eight, and get sixty-four miles as the distance they need to travel on their single gallon of gas. Realizing they can only travel seventeen miles, they sit at home sad and hungry. Was their math wrong? No, eight multiplied by eight does equal sixty-four. Their math and their data were right, but the system they put the data into was wrong.

These two illustrations show how mistaken calculations can create bad effects on a small scale. Now, let us imagine our equation two plus two equals four, becomes not only a real world problem but a matter of life and death. For example, you work as a raft guide and the boat you work on holds four people. You need four life jackets on board at all times, so if the boat breaks down everyone can escape to safety. That morning the employee who was responsible for loading the jackets got the name of your boat mixed up with another, and only put three on board. Now, even though you do have equipment on board to save lives, you only have enough to partially solve the problem. One plus one plus one does not equal four, and even though you have an answer - three - it is not *the* answer, and due to the error lives are lost when your raft sinks that evening.

Reality gives us no room to make mistakes in regards to very important things. What if a pilot messes up the calculation determining his flight path and has no computer to correct him? The plane, and all those in it, could hit a mountain or fall into the sea. What if an engineer made a mistake when she was calculating the amount of pressure it would take to crush the hull of a space station? All those inside of it could end up being crushed to death, and decades of work would be lost.

All parts of the calculations we make must be correct, otherwise we will make a mess out of our lives. The more important a thing is we are trying to figure out, the more horrible the loss when we mess up our equations or our measurements.

Now that we have the idea, let us change the type of problem we are trying to solve. We are no longer trying to figure out how much money we have, or how far our gas will take us. This time, we are trying to figure out what we are, where we came from, what it means to live, and how it is we should conduct ourselves. Right measurements are no longer numbers, they are the information we believe about life and the universe we have received from our teachers. Likewise, right equations are no longer mathematical formulas they are the religious, scientific, and philosophical systems that guide our thoughts and lives.

What happens when we get our facts about life or the system we plug the facts into wrong? Then, what we believe is wrong, and since what we believe determines our actions we behave in destructive and ignorant ways. Worse than the incorrect actions, is the fact we are using broken and errant systems to determine what is right and what is wrong. This means we could not only be doing the wrong things, but we can actually believe them to be the right ones.

When we have incorrect information about life, we do not just destroy and limit ourselves, but we cage and hurt the lives of others. In the worst cases, faulty belief systems and facts cause us to murder the innocent, hate the good, and forsake the precious. We must go to great lengths to make sure all we believe, all we think, and everything we view as true is not only comforting or popular but correct.

There is no way we can get our facts right until we name the things according to their nature, and not according to our cultural ideas of right and wrong, truth and error, good and evil. There is no way we can view life correctly unless we rid ourselves of all ignorance and illusion we possess. Those who do not realize their religious or philosophical system does not have all the answers will never look beyond it. Likewise, those who are not fearless will never have the ability to go against the people and powers that have taught them what to believe. Once we start getting our facts about reality right, then we can begin to understand what life really is, who we really are, and the best course of action to achieve any desired end.

If we do not have our facts right it does not matter if the system guiding our lives is the right one. We will still arrive at false conclusions just like our driver. It doesn't matter what you believe, what you think you know, what group you are a part of, or who you are. You must consider critically everything you are told and study broadly to see if it is so.

This is not the only reason for right measurements, they can also let us know the scale of the universe, the scale of humanity, and the scale of the walls we are trying to get beyond. Scale here means not only size but also potentials, effects, and value.

When we see the scale of the universe we begin to form an idea of what endlessness means, as well as the power of the elements that move within and without us. We also get an understanding of just how valuable life is. Value is determined by how precious something is to the one viewing it. Thus, I ask how valuable is life, the very thing granting all conscious things the opportunity to see and sense at all? It is priceless.

When we see the scale of humanity - its size, potentials, effects, and value - it is only then we can appreciate the life and personality possessed by all. We understand how there is nothing we cannot accomplish if we will choose to free our minds and fill them with wisdom. Also, we begin to see for the first time how the actions we take affect each and every thing around us, and why it is so important for us to be the best we can be.

When we see the scale of the wall dividing us and hiding the light from our eyes, then we can know how much it will cost to destroy these walls. What changes we must make within ourselves and habits, what friendships we must sever, and what hardships we must endure.

Then, knowing the scale of the walls, we can foresee the losses and trials we will endure, and by our foresight we can limit these as best we can. There is always loss when one destroys a social, moral, or personal illusion, yet the gains are always greater.

Knowing the scale of the universe, ourselves, and our obstacles keeps us from beginning the quest for freedom only to quit later. It also permits us to accept our humanity and the mistakes we are bound to make because of our inherent limits, while at the same time empowering us to rise above them.

This knowledge also lets us climb over the walls that move like viruses across the landscape of mind, without fear of failure. If we did not see the walls are small when compared to all we are capable of, we would begin to doubt our success and quit. If we did not understand the walls enclosing us are unnatural, we would not have the courage to tear them to the ground. If we did not glimpse the wonder, beauty, and wisdom filling our universe, we would not have reason to leave our fears and narrowness behind.

Knowing the right measurements and correct scale also gives us a right perspective. Perspective lets us know how big or small and far or near something is in relation to ourselves. Without right perspective, we would not know how to relate to the anything in our universe correctly.

As we move through life, if we take right measurements we will keep right perspectives. This in turn will keep us humble by making us mindful of how small we are in the vastness of reality, and how little we know about any of it. Meanwhile, it keeps us from feeling unimportant because though tiny in the universe, we see that on earth we are big. In this world we are all giants, each of us having the ability to accomplish our dreams, destroy illusions, help all we meet, and change the entire future of our race.

Keeping right perspectives helps us to know what is important in life and what is useless. We will not make big the small things others fill their lives with, neither will we make small the mountains others trample beneath their feet. We will also see what is precious, and what is harmful. In human culture, it is common to cherish most what we need the least, and to despise most what we really need. By having an accurate measure to judge the scale of all things, we will never be found trying to build a house with twigs.

Seeing things in the right way allows us to know how to move most efficiently through the troubles of life. You will see the nooks where you can escape the problems seeking to crush you, as well as the paths leading to the most refreshing experiences. Those with right vision do not waste energy by making hard and strenuous hikes to the tops of small things, nor do they sit lazily at the foot of life's grandest pleasures. When one has finally attained deep and correct insight, the way of action will always be known.

The benefit of right measurement also lets you know your strand of life connects to the web of the universe. This knowledge enables us to know the manner in which we should interact with all that exists. Knowing where you are in the web of reality, you will never find yourself lost. Knowing how to interact with all things you will not wound any you meet, forsake anything you need, or keep anything that will harm. Thus, you will get the maximum joy out of every experience.

With all the benefits of factual understanding laid out before us, only one final question remains - how are we to get this understanding? A right understanding of things can only be found by moving beyond the invisible boxes quietly containing our minds. Leaving what we already know - the understandings of our teachers, our texts, and our cultures - we must move into the unknown and study those things we have no understanding of. This prevents our wisdom and knowledge from being lopsided.

By making the contents of the whole universe our teacher, and fearless, open, honest, and relentless searching our friend, we can understand and discover anything. Imagine finding truths no one in our race has ever known before, and returning to teach them for the betterment of all. This is a wondrous goal, and as you seek to achieve it you are sure to find two things you have never found before; yourself and peace.

I have not yet mentioned a system where by right calculations can be obtained. The reason for this is all systems of thought should arise from the facts themselves. The facts should not be given their meaning or filtered out by our preexisting worldview, no matter how scientific or God-given we believe it to be.

By loving only truth, and clinging only to right information, you will automatically free yourself from misunderstandings and false beliefs. As we cast out all that is illusionary, we will simultaneously discover the only true system of knowledge and understanding in existence - reality as it is.

The goal of every person should not be to reinforce what they already believe but to test it, stretch it, squash it, and cut it until all untrue parts and pieces have been swept away. Our job is not to create a system of understanding, because then our understanding is the product of our human mind, and goes no deeper than human concepts and senses.

Instead of imagining truth and seeing the world as we wish it was our place is to find the nature of reality as it is. This means to understand things according to their construction, and then to harmonize ourselves with them. We did not create this reality, and so to understand it rightly our view of it must also be *uncreated* - it must arise from reality itself.

Just as the words of a book are to be understood according to what the author intended, and not according to the subjective fancies of the reader, so reality is to be understood according to the powers and principles that brought it into being and maintain its workings. This universe and all in it came about without any human intervention, and there is no human alive who can recreate it. Therefore, its true nature, and the way to understand this nature, must be equally uncreated otherwise it will be totally false. Only the infinite can measure and reveal the infinite. Those who insist on measuring what has no beginning or end by what has a beginning and an end, warp truth and distort reality.

By building systems of thought and belief upon the same eternal foundations upholding the universe, we will never find ourselves fighting against it. Those who set themselves against the ways of the cosmos will be crushed by it, just as those who dwell in illusion will have their fancies dashed by truth.

We do not *make* systems of truth we are parts *in* the system of truth. We have within us the ability to understand the grand movements of the universe, life, and humanity in all its parts. The goal is to realize *the System* and understand all of its parts, and our place among them, correctly.

Right measurements, plus right understanding, plus right method plus, wise action equals a wonderful personal experience that positively contributes to the whole web of existence.

Beyond What We Have Been Told

One day, Young Man was walking down a trail near the city, and on the distant horizon he saw what appeared to be the outline of Old Beauty. As he got closer it became clear it was her, but she was in a place the people of the city had told him never to go. Fearing for her safety, he got as close as he dared and called out, "You should not be there, it is dangerous!" Looking up from where she was digging, he could see she was wearing a very long necklace strung with onions, peppers, and garlic. Young Man's curiosity eventually overpowered his fear, and cautiously he made his way to her.

"What on earth are you doing here do you not know this place is evil?" Young Man said in a nervous and muffled tone. "Evil, that is a bunch of superstition created by a bunch of people who were too afraid to come over here and look around. Do you know why they call this place evil?" Young Man shook his head no as she continued, "It is because at night the land glows a soft green", Young Man interrupted her "You see evil spirits are in this place!" Old Beauty reached out and slapped him, "Use your head man! It is not spirits making this place glow green there is a bacteria abundant in the dirt of this area. If you take the dirt, boil it in water, and sift the grains out it makes a wonderful tonic to sustain your youth." "Why then are you wearing that odorous chain about your neck if it is not to ward off spirits?" Old Beauty slapped him again, "You just don't quit do you! I wear it to keep away mosquitoes."

Young Man was befuddled at how he had been misinformed by everyone in his life, seeing this Old Beauty asked, "Did I ever tell you about the brave little ant?" Young Man thought for a moment, shook his head no, and then she continued, "Once there was a colony of ants living in a tree. For hundreds of years they had marched up and down its leaves and limbs collecting food and building supplies, but over time it became forbidden to go above the leaves that kept the village hidden from the sun. One day a little ant thought to himself, "Why should I not go up there?" He thought hard and realized it was probably because there were birds that could swoop down and eat him, or the fact he could possibly be cooked by the sun. The little ant then decided to creep up there after sunset, when all the birds were sleeping. That night he made his way above the leaves and found, to his delight, clusters and clusters of the sweetest fruit."

"The next day, the little ant told the elder what he had found, and though the elder was dubious at first he eventually saw the good such an abundant amount of food could do for the colony. The elder sent his mightiest warriors and smartest scientists up the next night to collect and examine the fruit carefully. When they were done, they reported back that indeed the fruit was glorious and healthy beyond belief, and it could possibly even heal diseases they had never found a cure for. The

elder was elated and awarded the brave little ant with a house of his own. We should not disregard the wisdom of our elders, but we should always be aware they only know what they have been told, and no one has ever been told everything."

Chapter Seven

What is the foundation of our lives? This is a question few take the time to consider. Most of us were taught how to view the world as children, and since have had those ideas reinforced. Day after day, year after year, layer by layer the mix of thoughts making us what we are has been poured into our minds. We then build houses of thought and habit on these foundations, and never again ask, "Is this foundation solid?" However, if we are going to destroy the walls separating us from reality, this is the very question we must ask and answer.

We each are a house of ideas in which our consciousness, the part of us we see as being our self, lives. In this house, every idea supports another, interacts with another, and fits to another. First, are laid the ideas forming the foundation. These are our deepest beliefs about reality, life, the origin of the universe, and the nature of truth.

Upon this foundation we build the framework that will become our walls, hold our roof, and support our floor. This is our belief system, our moral ideas, our habits of action, and our goals for the future. Once we have finished constructing these, we set about boarding the walls up. We form ideas of good and bad, and by these we evaluate all things on the inside and outside of our homes.

Next, we put in our doors and windows. Through these we can see the world from inside our house of ideas and, after measuring them with our standards, determine what and who we are going to let in. Finally, we fill our house with our knickknacks of memories, symbols of importance, pleasurable ideas, as well as those things giving us comfort.

Once our house is built we let in the people from our own neighborhood - our culture and subcultures - and turn away those people and ideas we see as being *strange, incorrect,* or *bad.* We are very careful to let in only those things we are familiar with, those things that do not give us funny feelings. From inside our home, we look out at the world and see everything through our four-foot by two-foot window. Thus, all we see is being filtered through everything we believe and think.

This is not bad, it is just the way life functions, and all of us have the right to build our houses and decorate them however we would like. Yet, there is a great danger in this. What happens if our foundations are wrong? What happens if the things we have built our life on are not solid? We do not even like pondering the thought. In fact, humans avoid anything challenging what they feel is right or they enjoy. The reason for this is obvious. We think to ourselves, "If this small thing I thought was right is incorrect, then what else is wrong I believe to be right?" This idea is very distasteful to us, because it could lead to the realization that we have wrong measurements and a crooked foundation.

People are so attached to the way they view the world, because if it changes every other aspect of their lives will too. We hide away inside groups of people who think like us, watch movies and read books expressing the same ideas as us, and refuse to expose ourselves to anything different. If you change someone's view of life, you change the very essence of what they are. We are protecting our *self* - our personal image and our idea of who and what we are. *Self* is for most a priceless treasure, and is valued above all other people, places, or things.

This is the reason why people kill others who think, speak, or believe differently than them. People different than them are threats to the *self*, as well as its ideas of the world, and so need to be eliminated. The words and ideas of the ones killed were so powerful and new, they were a type of earthquake, a bringer of death to the little house of ideas. However, why do people fear earthquakes if they are sure their foundations are true? Those who are afraid to mercilessly check the foundations of their life have no real trust in them at all. If they did, they would eagerly set out to test them. If what you have built your life on is really truth, then measuring it with a true ruler will only reveal its strength.

However, is it possible our foundations could be weak and wrong? Is it possible the very ideas we have based our entire existence on are not even true? It is more than possible, it is almost certain. How can I be so sure? I know how our foundations are laid, and soon you will too.

Where do the ideas determining what we think about life, self, and those around us come from? They are taught to us by the segment of humanity we were born into - our culture. If I were born into a Christian home, then I would be taught the Christian way of viewing reality. The same is true for Communism, Taoism, Confucianism, Islam, Buddhism, Druidism, Atheism, and every other system of thought on earth. Even then, the world view I receive is not one held in common with everyone who comes from the same system of thought.

There are many variations of each and every way of thinking. Christianity is divided into hundreds of sub-groups as is Buddhism, Islam, and about every other worldview on earth. When you add in all the other factors influencing culture such as skin color, wealth, age, blood line, and personality it would be safe to say every human on earth has their own world view, sharing only a few core beliefs with those in their culture.

What then lies at the root of all these cultures? What is the number one driving force in the shaping of culture? It is a desire to measure up to the standards of those around you. However, who is it that sets these standards and determines when one fits in? The answer to this is found in humanities love for authorities, and is it our authorities in the end determining the direction and content of our culture. What is an *authority*? It is a person, book, or thing that determines what is right, wrong, good, bad, or otherwise in any people group.

In cultures using a holy book as the highest authority, it is almost always attributed to some supernatural person or given a supernatural origin. The people of India have a wealth of sacred texts functioning in this role, as do Muslims, Jews, Sikhs, and Christians.

In cultures where the authority is a person, their influence comes about due to a commonly held belief that they have some special attribute, understanding, or insight. Many native cultures function with the guidance from a holy man or priest. Even in our modern society when someone with letters after their name speaks most accept their words as though they were prophets.

The authorities of every culture are not supposed to be questioned, yet they influence every question one can ask about reality, and expect all to bow to their understanding. To an objective thinker, something that says, "I am the ultimate truth, but you can never test me to prove it" is a slap in the face of actual truth, and an enslaver of mind.

Even though religious and spiritual systems of thought are often the ones using an authority, all groups of people can fall into this trap. People want the meaningful things to be easy and obvious. They do not want to think too hard about them, because they have more pleasurable things to do. Authorities take advantage of such laziness by asserting they have the highest truth, and promise you can just trust them - trust them with your mind, trust them with your future, and especially trust them with your money.

Wherever you have a group of people there you will have some form of authority they can appeal to in order validate their culturally inherited point of view. Artists appeal to the masters, philosophers to the founders, scientists to the geniuses, and the spiritual to the prophets. However, the wise think for themselves.

The foundations of culture are laid on popular bodies of knowledge, and the backs of authorities who have mastered that body of knowledge. Then culture provides the foundation for the lives and minds of the people in it, and they in turn lay the same foundation in the minds of their children. Thus, ideas feed upon themselves and culture replicates itself in the mind like a weed.

How does this show the foundations most certainly contain flaws? It is the authorities that build the ways of thought and life for every culture on earth. These authorities disagree on many things. If the authorities, who are the truth masters for each culture, disagree with each other, then this leads one to an obvious conclusion - someone, if not everyone, is mistaken.

However, not only do the authorities themselves disagree with each other, wherever there is opportunity for an authority to be misunderstood, or wherever the manner of speaking is cryptic, there arises different interpretations of meaning. This leads to splits in the followers of that authority. Then you not only have an authority from one culture that is in contest with other authorities, you also have a group of people who swear they understand the words of their culture's authority better than others from their own system. Sunni and Shiite Muslims, Mahayana and Theravada Buddhists, and the almost endless versions of Christianity demonstrate this well.

With all this disagreement going on about what reality *really* is, what are the odds you were born or inducted into the one group of people on the face of the earth that has everything right? The odds are very slim, and who on earth is ready to entrust their life and future to blind chance?

How much time have you spent studying not only your culture's view of the world, but the views others have of it? I would say most people have not studied their own culture's understanding of the world, much less the insights given by other cultures. Those who have not studied widely and fearlessly all the forms of truth, and critically examined them, are only guessing or repeating what they have been told whenever they speak of ultimate truth. These should be gravely doubted from the start, and not unquestioningly believed in.

The main reason why the ideas we build our life on are untrue, is the fact we have let other people think for us. Each and every one of us are guilty of accepting what we have been told is truth at face value, without any objective and deep personal research into the matter. Easy, quick, and simple are the paths people love to take. If it takes hard work humans have a tendency to avoid it, and forsaking everything you think you know, and seeking the true of nature of reality is anything but simple, quick, and easy.

What then are we to do once we realize what we think is *real* and *true* most probably is not? Generally, there are two ways people respond. The first is to say, "I am *right* and everyone else is *wrong.*" The second, "nobody is *right,* and everyone can make up whatever idea they want and call it *truth.*" However, neither of these is wise. The first is full of pride and fear, and the second does not hold up under careful investigation. I think the best response to realizing how culture indoctrinates the minds within it is to step out of the current mental house, take it apart, and build it again.

Merely because the odds are slim everything is true, does not mean your system is totally false. It just means it has defects, or is missing some very important parts. What we must do is deconstruct our old house of ideas, and create a new one with a foundation resting upon solid rock and not concrete. What is the difference between these two? Concrete is a human creation and rock is not. The difference is having an understanding of reality based upon reality itself, and not upon some seemingly solid cultural concepts that have been mixed and poured by mortals.

Is it necessary to take apart the whole house we once had? Absolutely, we cannot fit all of reality in the small house culture has built for us, and the foundations culture has laid certainly cannot bear the weight. Reality is infinite, truth is infinite, and so too is the potential of humanity. We have to expand our house to hold all the new beauty to come, and if we do not we are doing something as silly as trying to fit the Amazon rain forest into an economy apartment.

However, there is some comfort. Merely because you take apart your old system of understanding does not mean you cannot reuse some of the lumber. All of humanity's world views are mixes of truth and error. Each of us must take them apart piece by piece, and critically examine them so we are only left with the truth. Once we have done this, we can incorporate the old parts, as long as they are true, into our new home of highest truth.

Merely trying to add new truth to an old way of thinking is like trying to add a stone wall onto a nylon tent, or a wooden roof to a buffalo skin wigwam. The two cannot mix, and the house will be exposed to harsh elements. Confusion, fear, doubt, and a horde of other things will come pouring in, and the mind will suffer greatly. Just as an army divided against itself cannot function correctly, neither can the mind that is split between wise and unwise ways of thinking.

It is by harmonizing yourself with the flow of the universe, and understanding how things work that we escape sorrow and find joy. It is like the little girl who has walked through the thorn patch for years, because it was the only path she knew would take her to the watering hole. One day her friend shows her a new path free of briars, and she gladly takes it. By knowing how the mind works, we can make it work correctly. By knowing what brings peace, we can pursue and obtain it. By knowing what creates suffering, we can reject and avoid it.

Deeper than all the speculations of humanity and the falsehoods of authorities, is an unshakable and true foundation. It is the system of life itself, how the mind and the universe naturally work and flow. It is the one path made up from many parts. Wisdom, selflessness, compassion, understanding, observation, reason, honesty, humility, fearlessness, and self-control are all parts of the way – the universal order.

Where reality came from, what it is, how it and its pieces work, as well as the best way to live must be explained with more than sacred assumptions, inherited superstitions, and human authorities. Pure wisdom free of dogma, discovered by deep personal exploration, established by extensive comparison, that is tested and expanded daily, is the only safe thing to build a life on. Whatever else we make the root of our existence binds the mind and turns living into slavery. The way of the universe is the way of wisdom, and those who build upon it shall never be moved.

Unity Through Wisdom and Logic

One day, Young Man came bursting into the tent where Old Beauty was sitting deep in reflection. Without even waiting to be acknowledged, he blurted out, "Where did the grove of fruit trees come from?" Slowly opening her eyes, Old Beauty looked curiously at her sudden guest and asked, "Why does it matter?" Young man replied, "I was in the market at the city and heard a group of men saying they were not planted by Heaven. They said the trees were deposited there by birds flying over the field after they had eaten from the fruit trees of the Village at the coast of the Island! I wanted to go and cut down the grove so those infidels could no longer eat of Heaven's bounty!"

Taking a breath to gather her thoughts, Old Beauty replied, "The origin of the grove is of great significance to the City. Did it happen by luck and bird droppings or did Heaven do it, and if Heaven did it which school of Heaven has the most accurate account? We should think deeply about these things, but while we are thinking about and debating them no one should be foolish enough to cut down the trees. They provide for the needs of human and beast."

Young Man's rage began to subside, he had never thought about it in just that way before. Seeing the light come on in the eyes of her friend, Old Beauty decided to make it burn brighter and asked, "Have you ever heard the story of the three camels?" Young Man shook his head no and so she began, "Once there were three camels traveling across the desert to a great city they had heard of. There all camels live in peace and never suffer want. Moving from oasis to oasis they were making good time and lacked nothing, until one day they came to where a river should have been and found only an empty bed."

Dirty, tired, and thirsty their tempers began to flare and two of them became engaged in the oddest of debates. The first said, "I am certain the water that ran here was as clear as crystal and almost as cold as ice." The second replied, "Well, the water was indeed cold and refreshing but there were minerals in it that gave it an extremely light red color, non-toxic but flavor enhancing." As the conversation went round and round the sun began to sink, the moon began to rise, and the third camel could stand the unenlightened banter no longer. Clearing his throat, the third spoke, "My friends, I am unsure as to whether the water was once clear or red, but has it ever occurred to either of you that you each arrived here at different times of the year, and though you drank from the same stream it appeared differently to each of you? Regardless, it is obvious the water once ran here, and now it is obvious it does not. If you two would like to stand here till you die of thirst bickering over unknowable details that is fine, but I am going to find water."

Chapter Eight

The nature of reality is at the root of each and every person's life whether they understand it or not. Where it came from, what it is, and how it works determines every aspect of our thought, action, understanding, and how we interpret all we sense. Any error in these areas will affect every thought in our minds, just as a crooked foundation will twist the entire house.

I have thought carefully about how one should approach this topic, and have decided wisdom and logic alone should represent the methods we use to understand reality, and form the platform for any conversation about it. This does not prevent us from having personal beliefs about the origin of the universe, it just means no matter what beliefs you have it is best to submit them to large doses of reason, wisdom, probability, and evidence.

The way we see reality must not be filtered through any internal ideas, likes, or dislikes. Reality should seen as it is, and measured according to what is real. What came first, the birth of all things, or the multitude of different explanations found in the varied authorities of each culture? Obviously, reality came first, thus any explanation of life must fit the events and interactions we now see taking place.

Not to say we are to discount and discredit the wisdom and experience of others on this topic, it just means we treat them as advisers, guides, and fellow humans rather than unquestionable manuals to reality, or divine rulers that must be obeyed.

By examining what everyone says with reason and logic, cross referencing it to the writings of other thinkers, comparing it to our personal experience, and caring only for truth, we open the door to achieving a view of reality beyond culture, belief, or personal desire. By boldly asking why, what, and how of everything, and then digging till we die or find our answer, we realize the truth. Truth is all that matters.

It is not about defending what we already believe, trying to prove what we have been taught, or keeping the ideas that make us comfortable. It is about finding the ultimate truths of reality and each thing in it, then applying those truths to our every moment.

If one does this, will they have confusion and disorder fill their mind? Yes, at the beginning there will be much confusion, pain, fear, and many will attempt to force you back into conformity with their simplistic and one-sided views. It is for this reason we covered the need to be fearless at the start, so we might have the courage and desire to push through the fears to find the glory and freedom awaiting us beyond our walls.

Those who seek truth can accept no human's word as the final answer. All ideas are fluid, and should be kept or rejected based not only on what evidence one has found thus far, but on the evidence one will find in the future. Those things that are proved time and again by broad and open study become guide points and those things that are proved untrue are let go.

No idea has immunity, no piece of information is shielded, and no period can ever be unchangeably placed at the end of our formulations of truth. Everything from the existence of a divine spirit, to whether or not the new vitamin the doctor suggests really worked, is tested in a merciless and tireless way. The more important the information is the deeper and more merciless we should analyze it.

It is a sad but true fact most of us do not want to find what is *really* true. We only want to be comforted in what we already believe, or to find a smart sounding reason to justify the aspects of ourselves we enjoy. This is one of the reasons why people only mingle with people of their own philosophical persuasion. Atheists very often only read atheistic books, thinking they are too wise to ever believe in the foolishness of a meta-physical realm. Likewise, do those fond of spiritual experiences avoid all things opposed to their particular world view. Conveniently, it is called *evil* by the shepherds of the flock, so they and their sheep can pass over it without giving it any serious consideration.

This tendency of people to flock to those of their kind is made worse by the *authorities* of the individual systems who bias the minds they teach with wrong perspectives, wrong information, or just outright lies. This happens in all schools of thought, be they monotheistic, pantheistic, polytheistic, atheistic, or otherwise.

None of this is the way of a truth seeker. Seekers are not hindered in their quest for truth by cultural taboos or shame games where the culture around them attempts to get them to conform their minds to the majority view points by calling them stupid, evil, or superstitious. The truth seeker sets their eyes only upon truth, and forever pursues it no matter who does not like their opinion, even if that person is themselves. Even when the seeker's world comes crashing down because they have discovered everything they have been taught is nothing but lies they push on, testing their new level of truth just as they did all prior levels. All information is tested until it is proven unquestionably true, untrue, or unknowable.

This is the guiding philosophy of my life. I have made it this way because when one builds a life unattached to personal concepts of truth, tempers all belief with logic, and all logic with wisdom, they are at peace with everyone wherever they go, because they are at peace with themselves. Not only this, they no longer do illogical things in the name of beliefs and ideas which cannot be objectively proven. Their minds are freed from the expectations and beliefs of those around them.

Our race - remember there is only one - fight and kill often over things that can be known only through faith. The problem is we treat our beliefs as though they are knowable like gravity. It is one thing to have deep personal faith in a way of life. However, it is altogether different to kill another human for not accepting the rules of an invisible world that cannot be tested or proven with anything besides the books or teachers of your religion. This applies to all religions and invisible things equally. To put faith in a system of thought is your choice and your right, but to kill another for not choosing as you have is murder.

Faith, better understood as trust, is a reasonable thing. Every day we trust we will not die when we leave our house, our water or food has not been poisoned by terrorists, and we can sleep without becoming the victim of a criminal. In reality, most just don't think about faith, but once we start thinking about it one quickly realizes there is no way of knowing bad things won't happen to us. We are so small and weak we must forever trust ourselves to the hands of chance, fate, or Heaven.

The ever present unknowns in life make trust in a good future logical, but murder is always illogical. Killing another human for unjust reasons is among the greatest acts of ignorance. Ending the life of another because they will not accept your perspectives on truth, your political agenda, or your will is unfair and selfish without end. If your way is really so much better, then why not present it with logic and proof instead of fear and force? Those who use fear, shame, guilt, one sided information and force to spread their ideas reveal their weakness and their lack of wisdom. What is good, wise, and logical does not attempt to manipulate the will, rather it educates and allows it the freedom to choose whatever it thinks is best; even if the choice is different than the teachers.

Murder is just one example of inhuman things done against humans who won't agree with the ideas of another. Any other evil action can fit here just as well, and if this wasn't bad enough, people do these evil things thinking they are doing holy acts, or somehow fulfilling the will of highest divinity. This is blindness.

How can one mercilessly kill the innocent in the name of one who gives life? How can I hate and murder in the name of one whose nature is compassion and mercy? How can I unjustly harm in the name of one who is a just healer? Such actions are blots upon the face of human potential, spiritual principles, and functional ethics. There are times when justice requires firm, unpleasant, and unflinching judgments, but to fulfill selfish want, manipulate the will, or harm the innocent in the name of justice is a disgrace without reason or excuse.

All of the different belief systems of the earth have created an almost endless number of thought houses. However, if we make the logic and virtue shared by all systems of enlightenment our base rather than our limited cultural ideas, we create a stable, just, and universal foundation. Then, the more specific elements of belief can be discussed without hate, murder, and undue pain for all involved.

Reason and wisdom must be the base of all our actions, because these show us how things really are. By observation and careful study, we can know how the things we see behave. We can see how understanding is better than prejudice, can taste how compassion is sweeter than hate, and watch how logical and wise actions excel emotional and hasty ones. One does not have to possess any faith at all to experience or observe these treasures, and this is but a drop of the bounty held in the store houses of wisdom and logic.

The life based upon logic and observation is immediately visible and accessible to everyone, but the *unseen* realms are closed to all except those who believe. Even then, these realms are seen only in the mind of the believer, and appear according to the descriptions contained in that believer's spiritual system. Thus, those who live a life based upon logic and wisdom can see the quality and consequences of their ideas immediately with their own eyes, while those who exclusively believe must accept another person's testimony about what matters most to them.

I am not undermining faith rather I am saying all faith should be built upon a solid and tangible foundation. Faith without reason is like having a blind and wounded elephant running loose inside the city mall - it produces great suffering and is very hard to calm down.

Ants, termites, bees, lions, dolphins, elephants, wolves, horses, and almost every animal living in a group does not harm the others in its group. In the dens, hives, schools, and herds of nature each individual knows their place, and lives a life that not only contributes to itself, but to the group in which it lives. This natural wisdom found in the other children of nature far surpasses the thoughtless ways humans interact with each other. Our world is divided and decaying, because we have no understanding about what is best for ourselves. How much less do we understand what is best for all living creatures on the earth?

Humans watch greedily to accomplish only what is best for themselves not caring for other forms of life or even our own kind. This selfishness has painted our world in terms of *us* and *them*. *We* are right, and *they* are wrong. *We* deserve the best, because *we* are the chosen and *they* deserve only death because *they* are demonic and vile. *We* are the smartest, so *we* only should be allowed to teach, and *they* are so foolish even their right to speak should be taken away. Again and again, deeper and deeper, does this pathetic *us* and *them* mentality divide. In the end we hate people we do not know, and hurt those who are just like us, because we think they are different.

If only we could see we are not divided. What affects the greatest of us affects the smallest, and when any human dies unnecessarily due to the evil mind of another all humanity dies a little. By degrees, the worth and virtue of humanity is raised or lowered daily by the actions each of us have taken that day. We are not divided we are all part of one human family. It is not until each of us is taught compassion and unity that we can learn or use any other truth reality has in store for us.

This is why we make what is visible and provable the foundation we build the rest of our thought house upon. It lets us see how our fate is bound up with the earth, and each of those things it contains. To flow and harmonize with all that is seen is to be in union with the forces that brought it into being. Observing what does the greatest good for all, and doing it leads the mind into the center of wisdom. From there the importance of peace, kindness, forgiveness, honor, mercy, and justice are clearly seen.

This is a sharp contrast to what happens when you let an authority define what is right and wrong based on some invisible reality or hidden wisdom they alone can see. Where there is no individual and critical thought, ignorance, evil, and suffering abound. If you have complete faith in an authority, they can make you commit any number of evils, and you will think you are doing right.

The authorities are the ones who taught you the definitions of right and wrong, and when you measure your actions by their standards you *feel inside* and *know in your heart* your actions are good and holy. We must personally seek the highest levels of truth, and then govern our own minds according to its standard. If you do not rule your own mind by truth, another will rule it for you so you can build their dreams for them. The pages of history overflow with examples of this.

Any idea or habit that can be proven false and harmful by wisdom and logic ought to be abandoned by the mind possessing it. Nevertheless, the choice to live in the real world or a world of illusion is a personal decision each of us must make for ourselves. If someone prefers illusions to reality it is their right to do so, just as it is the right of others to believe and act according to their best or preferred understandings, as long as it does not unjustly harm or limit another.

Nothing must become a spiritual obligation enforced by law, fear, or harm, no matter how good or bad any of us believe it to be. No other human on earth has the right to take away a drop of freedom from another, much less the freedom from where all others arise - freedom of thought.

There is a beautiful harmony that exists among all living and non-living elements of our universe. This harmony arises from logical principles that apply to all things equally. If humanity could agree on the most basic principles of wisdom and logic, and actually apply them, our world would become just as harmonious, efficient, and beautiful as the realm of nature.

This harmony would be like a fertile soil where the seeds of communication could take deep root, and grow into flowers of understanding that would beautify the lives of all living things. If we could at least accept with kindness and understanding those who do not agree with us, as well as their right to disagree, we would revolutionize our world. It is for the betterment of humanity by the spreading of truth and understanding that any form of knowledge should be taught. If humanity is only demoralized and degraded by your knowledge, then you are a cancer and not a cure.

Wisdom and logic together compose the system to base our lives on. This doesn't mean we are abandoning or betraying our faith, because the purpose of faith is to connect us to a pure eternal reality. If that reality is only a comfortable illusion created by a corrupt and temporary mind, then our faith - our trust - should be put elsewhere.

No religion or philosophy on earth is made worse by having a firm grasp on reality. Are not wisdom, logic, and understanding the greatest attributes of any divine being, and the highest goal of humanity? If humans are spirits, should we not conduct ourselves as the holiest spirits do? If we are only material, should we not behave in the same orderly and logical way the rest of the material world does? Truth is what gives any system of thought its value. It does not matter what you think or believe, the pursuit of truth, and the liberal application of it to your life, should be your focus.

As humans, we ought to strive to replace all that is imaginary with deep, honorable, and objective truth. Traditions, beliefs, actions, and all illusion ought to be washed away, so we can act in harmony with the way things really are. All things not visible or empirically provable ought to be subjected to critical analysis, and if they are found to be unlikely, incorrect, or unwise, we need to seek a better and more accurate explanation. This is true for all systems of thought be they philosophical, scientific, or religious.

Today, humanity thinks we know it all, when in reality we are like babies nursing from the breast of two sisters called *The Vastness of the Universe* and *All Knowable Things*. No doubt we have a great deal of knowledge about a great many things, but when we compare what we know to the scale of the universe, we find we do not know much at all. We are so full of certainty there is no room in our minds to learn, and so our parts of knowledge prevent us from acquiring more of the whole.

The powers of science cannot prevent death, the medicines and chemicals we make are second rate compared to the construction and healing properties of those occurring naturally, and our most complex creations cannot even compare to the complexity found in a blade of grass. We are children trying to raise ourselves to the wisdom contained in the book of the natural world.

We cannot know anything correctly until we accept we do not have perfect knowledge. We think because we have named a bunch of things, and can predict their behaviors, we are a wise and great race. The truth is we are small and in need of much learning. We have not even mastered the most basic things of life - love, beauty, peace, mercy, forgiveness, truth, honor, justice, logic, and understanding. Therefore, it does not matter how fast our computers can process, or how far our space ships can go. If we do not master the most important, the most impressive is made worthless, because we will only kill ourselves with its wonders.

The hardest thing for any system of thought is to accept its limitations, and even a system based purely upon logic has these. There are places where reason and logic cannot go, because there is not enough information. Logic can take you from A to Z, but it cannot take you where there is no alphabet. The information we cannot know, due to the limits of our tools, the smallness of our size, and the shortness of our lives, logic and reason cannot reveal to us. Those who force a limited mind to reveal an unlimited answer by considering inadequate information produce only smart sounding assumptions reason herself declares illogical.

There is much we have learned, and yet the simplest truths are the ones we cannot or do not want to grasp. There is so much about our race and reality that is still a mystery. If we will be logical and wise we can create a future where all of humanity lives at peace with one another, and all the resources we once used for war can be used to reveal truths we have never dreamed of. When wisdom, logic, and truth are united in the human mind, all of the actions and ideas we have will be firmly grounded in the known while pointing profoundly into the unknown. Then, all the wars that come about because of false certainty about unknowable realities will cease.

Wisdom and logic must become the base of our existence, because these deal in real ways with real things everyone can sense and measure. Reason and understanding let us build a sure and solid foundation for our life. However, building upon intangible ideas and beliefs causes us to misunderstand reality, and prevents us from knowing anything as it really it. Belief as a basis for action causes us to see each other as devils, when realizing our common humanity is more important than ever.

Principles of the External World

One day, Young Man traveled from the City to the Village in order to get some fresh produce. To do so, he had to pass through the Forest, and as he made his way through the vibrant wood, a question suddenly arose in his mind, "By what principles does this reality work?" He felt confident Old Beauty could tell him, and as soon as he got back to the City, he ran up the Mountain to ask her.

He was filled with such excitement that again he burst into the tent without announcing his arrival, but this time Old Beauty was bathing and not reflecting. Even though she was not a young woman she was very beautiful. At the sight of her Young Man's face flushed red, his mouth filled with apologies, and his feet pedaled backwards towards the door. Old Beauty accepted his apology, finished her bath, dried herself, and readmitted her guest, curious as to what had filled him with such hurry.

Young Man explained to her what had happened, asked her how reality worked, and then peered at her as though she was going to tell him the secrets of everything. Appreciative of his respect she began, "Reality is like a bottomless ocean, no matter how deep we go we will never get to the bottom. Nevertheless, it is still like unto an ocean. As an ocean fills, evaporates, takes shape, and changes moment by moment, so are all things in reality constantly shifting and changing. Whenever one disturbs the waters, their disturbance spreads throughout the whole, and no part of the ocean exists in isolation from the rest; even though it is made of billions of tiny individual pieces. It really exists though its size and nature causes us to misunderstand, and if you took half of it and poured it into another basin it would make another set of waters just like itself. Throughout all its waves, there are no divides, and all apparent divides are merely limited minds painting their limits onto the limitless deep."

Chapter Nine

Most of us are so lost in our ideas of how the world is we are completely disconnected from the way things really are. We filter all we see through whatever authority we trust the most. Thus, we live not in reality, but inside a world made from other people's words and our personal opinions.

The harm this causes is obvious to all who will open their eyes and see. Millions and millions of people are walking around suffering, hurting, and dying due to the actions they are taking; actions taken because of the way they understand the world.

Most of this suffering could be prevented if we would all learn how reality really is and then act in unison with the principles governing the universe. Cause and effect are always interacting to create our world. If we do not like the effects we are feeling, or the circumstances we are living in, then it is time to change the erroneous thoughts and actions leading us to our state of suffering. Change can only be made by seeking, understanding, and harmonizing with the true nature of reality.

How are we to find the true nature of reality? The writings of others are a good place to start. We can absorb their wisdom, avoid their mistakes, and be inspired by their experiences. However, this alone is not good enough. Without a personal grasp of how things really are, we will absorb not only the wisdom and truth in others, but we will also take in their ignorance and mistakes.

To truly experience reality, all we have to do is lay down all the theories, stories, and ideas we have been taught *about* reality, and realize we are immersed in the real at all times. Reality is not hidden from the eyes of the master, the beginner, or even the fool. Everywhere we look and travel there is timeless reality in all of its massive and delicate beauty. To find the nature of reality, one must set aside prejudice, pride, the illusion of knowing, and take a seat under a tree. If you have the ability to do this physically as you read the following, it will increase your understanding. However if you cannot, the visualization of being seated under a tree is good enough.

To find reality one must leave all books and people at home, no matter how much we love them or how much they may have helped us in the past. After leaving all external influences behind, we can then release all thoughts about the world others have planted in us, and simply watch the elegant workings of the natural world.

While seated beneath our tree, what we are going to consider are only those things we can see. The invisible will not be used to explain the visible unless there is incontrovertible evidence an invisible element is affecting the material world. Do you see angels or have you objectively verifiable evidence of their working? No? Then do not use them to explain your world. Do you see demons, spirits, gods, or jinn or have objective evidence of their working? No? Then do not use them to explain your world. Turn everything you have been taught, and everything you think you know, into a theory that is going to be tested by the reality surrounding you.

This may seem extreme to some, and no doubt sounds like a sin to others, but if we do not test and retest all we have been taught, how can we know it is true? Likewise, if we have not tested and retested the ideas others call true, how can we know if they are wrong? Believing in something unreal does not make it real, and hope is not a spell one can use to get the things they hope for. If we allow belief, hope, fear, guilt, reward, or punishment to control our minds, how can we profess to be free? Many minds are dominated by the ideas of the society they are born into. They are too terrified, depressed, or lazy to free themselves and look behind the walls to see what is really there.

If what we have been told is true, then open research will only cause its truth to shine more brightly. If our truth turns out to be a lie, it is better for us to know now than to devote our lives to an illusion. The pain one feels when they realize what they have been taught is errant or incomplete is tremendous. Yet, it is nothing compared to the pain of realizing on your death bed you have spent your life building an illusion, and submitted your freedom to the rule of fables and fools. This is true for the fool, the scientist, the philosopher, and the religious person alike. No one is immune to being taught lies, and no one is beyond being accidentally misled by well-meaning people or themselves.

As a scientist, knowledge gained by observation is the highest form of wisdom. Thus, to test again the foundational theories of reality will only improve the quality and quantity of one's scientific understanding. As a philosopher, one's purpose is to find the purest expression of reality by questioning every answer, and testing the foundations of all questions. Thus, questioning and testing all they know will only bring philosophers closer to their goal, and make them more of what they aspire to be. Religious people too should not be afraid to critically examine all they have been taught about God, life, and eternity to see if what they believe is really true. After all, what type of obedience would be more pleasing to a just and wise God - obedience out of fear and ignorance, or obedience that flows freely out of understanding and appreciation for Divine justice and wisdom? Is it better to be a slave to a lie all of your life, or to free yourself from all lies and truly live? How horrible would it be to realize what you have been causing others to devote their life to an ancient superstition and not the will of God? As for fools, they need to learn any truth they can before their foolery robs them of life and joy.

All who truly want to live must question everything they live by. If they do not do this they are not living their life, they are life forms with the mind of another in control of their body. Those do not ask why, and do not know the reasons why they do the things they do are slaves. They dare not question, and if they do question they are beaten by their master, their uninformed conscience, and the other slaves. Mental freedom is the right of every human as is mental slavery. All deserve to be given the tools, information, and liberty to decide which they will choose. No one will give you your freedom you must reach out and take it yourself. Truth is the only path that can lead to freedom. Truth is a correct expression about the nature of reality. Thus, we have returned again to our tree in the field, and the reason why we are sitting under it in the first place.

The first question most people ask about reality is, "Where did it come from?" but a better first question is, "What is it and how does it work?" If you do not know what a thing is, or how it functions, anything you say about where it comes from is a blind guess that is almost definitely going to be wrong.

What then is reality? Total reality is made from several parts. The first part, called *material reality,* is the external material universe our senses convey to us. Even our bodies and their chemistry are a part of this world. This part of reality was not and is not created by me, though I can alter it. Neither does it need me to exist, though I can change its form. The material world was here before I was born and will be here long after I die.

The second part of reality, *mental reality,* is the perception of the material universe, and the understandings about it, created in the minds of the creatures living in it. This part of reality is unique to every individual creature. It is influenced by personal experiences and beliefs, the society and environment one is born into, the capacity of the individual's mind to understand, and how much of their natural capacity is being used.

In this chapter, we are going to discuss the principles of material reality. Those of the mental reality will be discussed in the next chapter. Also, the reader may have noticed I said reality is made of several parts but only listed two. I do this because I am not equipped to affirm, classify, or deny in a definite and objective way the realm of the metaphysical. I will not set forth my ideas about what is beyond the realm of sense as undeniable truths. The principles I will be discussing about the material and mental realities are beyond any doubt, and I will not detract from them by speculation.

What is the material reality? Material reality is made up of each and everything thing existing, as well as the nothingness between and beyond it. It is the rocks, dirt, clouds, stars, plants, animals, and the components that make them.

This material reality, although it seems solid, is not really material at all. It is different types of energies that have bonded in unique and orderly ways according to their nature. Water is a set number of electrons, protons, neutrons, and other subatomic particles that have bonded. Its behavior and appearance are due the type of bond these energies have. All things really are just energy; it is not some superstitious new age non-sense, it is the way things really are.

Plants, animals, and people are made up of systems that are themselves made up of cells. These cells are composed of mineral and chemical compounds arranged in a highly organized way, so they produce life and consciousness. These minerals and chemicals are made up from atoms, that in turn are made up from small charges of positive, negative, and neutral energy - protons, electrons, and neutrons - that are themselves bound by even smaller charges of energy.

What applies to living things also applies to inorganic things. Minerals, elements, chemicals, and all inorganic matter break down into atoms formed by interconnected energies. All matter is only bundles of energy that appear solid.

These energies do not seem to obey the same principles governing the larger objects and life forms they make up. In order to understand the subatomic world, we had to create another school of physics, new theories, and accept the fact there are limits to what we can know of this micro-world; at least with our current understanding and technology.

Even though the physical world we see is complex, and seems to behave in different ways depending on what part you are looking at, it is still one indivisible whole. The proton in an atom contained in the diamond used to make a watch is the same type of energy at the center of everything else in existence. We should always remember this to avoid making the mistake of isolating the individual things we are studying, as well as ourselves, from the rest of the universe.

The amazing complexity of the material world is far too broad to even attempt to cover in this chapter. There are people who have made specific areas of study the purpose of their life: astronomy, geology, physics, anatomy, chemistry, mathematics, biology, and meteorology being just a few of these. This chapter does not intend to discuss all the details about reality, all of which no one knows, but rather some grand principles applying to all things.

This at first may seem like a hard thing to do, but it is not. The key lies in understanding all things in the material world use the same building material - atomic energy. They vary in appearance and behavior only because the quantity and organization of these energies differ from thing to thing. We can understand this by comparing it to automobiles. Most all vehicles have a frame, engine, wheels, lights, windows, and seats, but the ways these things are put together make each vehicle unique. A 1957 Chevy obviously differs from a Caterpillar dump truck.

It is a firm understanding of the principle I call, "*Common Composition but Differing Form*" that enables us to learn something about everything, whenever we learn a little bit about anything. When we have understood the construction and behavior of one thing, we can understand the construction and nature of everything; at least in regards to it basic attributes. To clarify this, think again about our automobiles.

By understanding what the 1957 Chevy is, how it works, and how to operate it we can understand much about the same aspects of the dump truck. By mastering thoroughly what they have in common, we can more easily master their differences. The same holds true for reality. There are some basic principles applying to everything, and if we learn these we will be better prepared for anything.

The Principles

Impermanence

Our first universal principle of reality is the impermanence of all things. Impermanence means something is temporary and always changing. All things in the universe are in a state of constant change. Everything in existence was once something else, and is on its way to becoming yet another thing.

Our bodies began as packets of biological data held in the loins of our parents. Then this data combines to make a cell, which makes other cells, which make a fetus, which becomes a baby which grows into adulthood and eventually returns to the elements it was constructed from. Then, these elements are absorbed and become part of a sprout, that turns into a plant, which eventually returns to the elemental compounds it is made from, and so the cycle goes endlessly. I am speaking here of the objective reality and not about any form of reincarnation or transmigration some faiths believe the soul to take. All that is alive will die if things do not keep this from happening, and once dead it will be used again by the mechanisms of life.

Just as the living things on earth cycle, so do the material ones. Molecules of water change from ocean waves cloud vapor, to rain, to creeks, to rivers, to oceans, and around again. As it is with water, so it is with all other parts of the material world. Everything is caught in a cycle of change.

Nothing now seen is everlasting, no matter how glorious or beautiful its current form may be. Even the sun that gives earth light, if time does not somehow abruptly end, will someday burn out, explode, and return to the energies that made it.

All humanity would be happier if they would take firm hold on this principle. If we did, we would be able to move beyond the greed and self-pampering now dominating the world at large. We work, oppress, pay, borrow, and steal so we can amass a bunch of sense objects and have pleasurable experiences. Is this not a waste of valuable strength and peace? We cannot keep anything, not even our own lives. The stuff we seek to make us happy decays, as do the senses that let us experience them. If we have not taken the time to obtain knowledge of the eternal, despair will be our only remaining possession.

We do not like to think about the impermanence of reality, because it brings us face to face with our mortality. This is why we must be fearless. By boldly looking into the mouth of death, we learn some of the most important secrets about how to live. We do not worry as much about getting rust and rot prone possessions, or pampering our decaying bodies.

This principle also helps us to enjoy the material world to its fullest extent. When I get my new shiny thing, I know it will soon scuff, spoil, and break. Knowing this, I do not become attached to its newness, and so I do not suffer when it is gone. I do not lash my child because he scratched my car, because scratches are bound to happen. I do not abuse my dog when it chews my shoes, because they would have soon been worthless anyway.

By releasing our attachment to the forms and happenings of the world around us, we put our happiness beyond their reach. The one who understands the brevity of beauty is empowered to relish the present joy, and let it pass away without losing their peace. They obtain freedom from greed and materialism, not by mysteries, but by understanding the nature of things. They know time and functionality are limited so they wisely use all things neither wasting nor hording them.

Cause and Effect

The next principle we are going to discuss is cause and effect. All objects and information our senses encounter arise from specific causes, and give birth to effects that in turn become causes.

Things in our universe do not happen by magic. For everything in our material realm, there is a sequence of specific actions causing it to take form, maintain form, and dissolve. Examples of this intricate cause and effect are found everywhere around us. The loaf of bread sitting in your local grocery store did not just appear on the shelf one day. Store managers, bread company owners, factory workers, truck drivers, farmers, machinery, seeds, and sun all took actions causing the bread loaf to be where we see it.

As with bread, so it is with all things. Cars, trees, houses, rocks, all we look at and interact with on a daily basis are produced by a series of events causing them to be where and what they are today. Without action nothing happens, no work is done, no progress is made, and nothing comes to pass. By fully realizing this, we can analyze our lives and figure out why it is our life has turned out the way it has. Why am I always broke, why did this break, why can I not sleep, why am I gaining weight, why am I sick, why do I hurt, how did I end up in the circumstances I am in, and a million other questions can be answered by slow and careful reflection on how the principle of cause and effect has been at work in our lives and reality.

Reflecting on our lives in this way also helps us to understand how to move forward in life. By flipping the above process, considering what actions I need to take to get where I want to go instead of considering what actions I took to get me where I am, we can answer many otherwise puzzling question. How to get more money, gain muscle, and an unlimited number of other questions can be answered by reasoning in this way.

Millionaires did not get where they are now by rubbing a bottle, and asking the genie inside to answer their wishes, neither did they achieve their status by pure positive thought. They, and many others, took actions that eventually led to the realization of their dreams. By mastering ourselves, understanding how others work, and understanding our world we can accomplish our highest aspirations without becoming unrealistic.

Finally, I would like to mention that choosing not to act is itself an action. There is nothing we can do to escape influencing the world around us. If we sit on our butt and do nothing, this too is an action, and it creates an endless chain of consequences.

We are all members of this world, and each thing we do while living in it drastically changes reality. This is why doing all we can to cure ourselves of ignorance is important. Wise actions bring good consequences, while foolish actions bring bad ones. We must think carefully about how our choices alter our lives, and the lives of those around us, because choice is a power like no other.

Interdependence

Cause and effect naturally lead us to consider the principle of interdependence. Everything you see could not have come into its current form, continue in its current form, of even pass out of its form without a multitude of other things helping it along the way. For example, an acorn needs water, sunlight, good soil, good biology, and good luck in order to become an oak. However, in order to have water one needs rain, in order to have rain one needs heat, in order to have heat one needs the sun, and in order to have the sun one needs atomic fusion. All things are interrelated, and need other things to exist.

It would be incorrect to say in order for anything to exist, everything must exist. Cases of extinct plants, animals, and human empires show things can forever die, and reality will continue on without them. However, the existence and fate of all things on earth is hopelessly intertwined. Think about the economies of nations, the ecosystems of nature, the structure of living cells, and the organisms cells make. Everything needs something else to exist.

Where would the body be without the heart? Where would the heart be without the body? Where would the grass be without the sun, the gazelle without the grass, or the lion without the gazelle? Again, all things are interrelated and could not exist if they were totally isolated.

The extreme number of connections between all things reinforces what we learned from cause and effect, and again reveals to us why we should be concerned with the actions we take in life. Our influence upon the world, and our world's influence upon us, is almost endless.

There is no *greater* or *lesser, better* or *worse.* Things and people only differ in nature, and have different effects on the world. By comparing and contrasting, we can learn much, but we should not fall into the trap of evaluating something by another thing. We need to understand and evaluate things according to their own nature, and by the effects they produce. Generalizations made from stereotypes have little value, and to judge a million things by the actions and nature of one individual is not wise.

When we understand interdependence as we should, we see right action is not just an empty religious mandate followed to give our lives meaning, or a virtue we strive for in order to keep a good self-image. When every part of the system is working rightly, every other part of the system is nourished and granted the ability to function in its best and highest capacity. When things correctly fulfill their role, there is peace and health for all.

Independent Nature

At this point, it is important we discuss another principle that balances the idea of interdependence; the principle of independent nature. Even though each and every part of reality needs other parts in order for it to function, they are still individual parts with their own unique and separate identity.

Some see the way all things on earth work together, and think the oneness of everything is not metaphorical but literal. There are many philosophies and religions that have espoused this view, but it is not the case at all. All things in reality function *like* one giant organism, but they are not *one* living entity. Each and every object has its own structure, existence, and place in space and time. Even though it needs other things in order to take form, to exist, and to dissolve, it still has an individual identity. Let us consider a few examples to make this more understandable.

Find a plant and ask, "Is the plant the soil?" The soil has elements of plants that have died in it, the plant takes the nutrients from the soil into itself and turns them into its cells, and the plant could not live without the soil, yet they are still independent of one another. The soil is non-living and much less complex than the plant that lives, reproduces, and conducts photosynthesis. The two do not have the same atomic organization even though they are made of the same energy; they are not one thing.

While still sitting there in front of the plant, ask another question, "Am I the plant?" This may seem like nonsense it is a good way of showing both you and the plant have individual and separate existences. Very obviously you are not the plant. You had to travel from where ever you were at to sit in the same area as the plant. Also, you each have different atomic and cellular constructions, different forms, different chemical processes, unique life cycles, and unique deaths. You and the plant are not two sides of the same coin rather you are two different coins in the bank of the universe.

Picture reality as a car, the car is one total thing, but it is composed of many individual things. It needs each of them in order to function in the way it was designed to. You can take parts off the car, like a tire or a muffler, but separated from the vehicle they cannot fulfill their purpose. The whole only works if all the parts are there, and the parts fulfill their role only when they are connected to the car. It is not that the radiator is the same thing as the tire, each are independent parts. They are two different parts sharing a common whole and contributing to its workings.

Even though all things in the universe are made from the same basic energetic building blocks, they are not all the same thing. Trees, rocks, birds, dogs, cats, sun, moon, water, fire, earth, all material things living or non-living are encompassed by one massive reality where they play their part. If we lose sight of this we begin to come up with strange theories that cannot be objectively proven, and end in misunderstanding rather than wisdom.

Each thing behaves as it does, because of the way its materials interact with each other and the external world. The materials are formed from delicately balanced packages of energy that bond with other energies based on their atomic structure. Each form you see - tree, bug, cloud, car, or clown - occupies its own spot in space-time and has personal identity and substance.

Once we understand this, we can understand in a true and practical way how each thing works, why it works, and how it affects the whole. This principle also prevents us from changing a solid and tangible world, where things behave the way they do because of their unique construction, into an ethereal world where nature is manipulated by magic and spirits. Realizing everything is not literally one undivided whole causes us to realize our individually, as well as that of others, and helps us to know the actions we must take as individuals to keep all things in good working order.

Actuality

There are philosophies that think the universe, and all its contents, are created by our thoughts. Even though mind plays a large part in shaping reality, and how we view it, reality is not some illusion created exclusively by our mind.

Each thing we see, though it is received, interpreted, altered, and experienced in our mind, exists outside of our mind as an actual and substantial thing. Mount Everest is a thing outside of me. It existed before me, continues on in spite of me, and will exist after I die as long as something doesn't destroy it. The name the mountain is known by is created by mind, and the vision I have of it exists only in my mind, but the thing itself is external to me and real.

When archeologist discover lost cities, ships, or treasures they are not finding things their minds created days before. The hidden items were created from materials existing before they did, and by people who lived before the explorers we born. When the makers of these items died, the things they made continued to exist and eventually were lost in time. Later, these creations were found by others who had no idea what they looked like, or where they were placed, and at times did not even know they existed at all.

For example, the person who found the *Dead Sea Scrolls* was not looking for them, and did not even know they were there, yet random events caused them to be found. Likewise, the early Spanish explorers who ventured into the Americas did not create the native peoples, the complex native architecture, or their finely crafted treasures, by some semi-divine mental power. Those people and things already existed and were *found* - though they were never lost - by the Spanish. The Spaniards desire carried their bodies, which housed the tools of perception, into unknown parts of reality.

Whenever the people who made the relics died, the relics did not disappear showing us they were not a psychic projection. If they were, they would have vanished when the mind creating them died. This is further proven by the events with the *Dead Sea Scrolls*. How could they have been created by the mind who found them when that person had no idea they even existed? Then, there is the story of the Spaniards. They could not have mentally created the wealth, art, and culture of the peoples they met in America, because their existence was unknown to the Spanish.

When people are born the universe is not created, and when people die it does not disappear. The material universe is real, it is not a powerful projection of any mortal's mind. Yes, we shape our world with our minds, but it is not by some subconscious creation chant.

The personality of every human is controlled by their mind. Our perceptions of reality, and the memories we have of those perceptions, exist only in our mind, and all human actions begin in, and flow from, mind. Nevertheless, the world outside of us is an external reality that does not need any created consciousness in order to exist. When we get our minds around this idea, we stop trying to *believe* our hopes into existence. We begin to seek out the way the universe is, and then take actions that will create the outcomes we desire in the material world.

We do not sense even a quarter of what is happening, and our mind fills in certain aspects of what we sense with what we expect or believe should be there, but these truths do not reveal that we are mini-gods. Rather, they just show us our senses are limited, and that we need tools instead of psychic powers to build the reality we desire. Luckily, our mind is the greatest tool in the known universe, and though it doesn't give us the power to be reality shaping demigods, it enables us to understand reality as it actually is and to find our actual place in it.

Replication

If you have ever seen a dandelion flower ready to sow its seed, you have seen a flawless example of the principle of replication. Beginning as a seed, it grows up into a plant, and then scatters hundreds of other seeds that are replicas of it as far as the wind carries them. This self-replication, or like from like, is found throughout the material world; being especially true concerning living things.

Whenever we plant an apple seed do grape vines come up, or when we melt gold do we get a smelting pot full of silver? When horse breeders mate purebreds do they get donkeys, or when we crush diamonds do we get copper powder? Things produce other things like unto themselves.

When we introduce violent actions into the waters of reality, do we really expect something besides violence to return? When we do nothing at all should we expect to get something in return? Reality is never haphazard in the way it moves. When we put a certain thing in, we will get more of that kind of thing in return. We are all prone to cry about reality being unfair but the opposite is true; reality is totally fair, giving us only the fruit of our actions. Never does reality give us a penny more than we have earned.

At first this sounds like a great deal. I work hard and do my thing, and the natural world gives me the fruit of my labors and all are happy. However, there is a dark side. Though reality always gives back what was put into it, it makes no distinction between those who planted the seed, and those who happen to be in the field whenever the seed ripens and bears fruit. Picture a giant pool of water the whole of humanity is swimming in. If I inject a red dye into one end of the pool, will the other end remain unaffected? No, the dye will slowly diffuse until it tints the entire body of water red. What is true of the pool is true also of reality.

When actions are taken that are out of harmony with the natural flow of the universe, the abnormalities caused by it are felt by all. When someone works hard to gather wealth, reality honors their efforts and gives them the fruit of their deeds. However, when the same person begins to choose to cling to their wealth and refuses to give the poor even the smallest gift, reality honors their choice and the poor suffer.

Just as people unwisely use wealth, so unwisely act in many other ways. This is why we must understand the principle of replication, and the total connectedness of reality. When I see how my actions and their outcomes are reproduced in others, I begin to grasp the reason why I need to make sure the actions I am taking are of the best quality.

In the natural world, hot and cold air start an orderly and reasonable turn, only to produce a whirling titan destroying all in its path. The tornado will move along a course until it has run out of energy, and then it will diffuse and become again the friendly wind. As it is with tornadoes, so it is with human actions. We must not let our actions become unintelligent powers wrecking all they contact. We should be balanced and gentle like the processes that give to the earth its bounty, and that the earth in turn shares with all upon it.

Where does the effect of our actions end? For example, let us say one day a man angers me and I kill him. When is it the consequences of my action come to an end? The answer is never. By killing the man, I have set into motion a chain of events that will alter every moment thereafter. He will not be there for his kids, and their lives will be changed because of his absence. The changes that take place in their life will in turn affect the lives of everyone they meet, and then these lives will go forth and affect others; the chain is unending.

It is like knocking over an endless row of dominoes. Once you have taken action and knocked over the first, the dominoes never stop falling. If the world is ever going to be a paradise, then all those who live on it will realize the endless consequences of their actions, and only act in ways yielding sweet and healing fruit. Observe the material reality, and watch how your actions alter it, and how the happenings in it alter you.

Relativity

Words like big, small, tall, short, near, far, light or heavy are comparative terms - they only tell us anything when the object they are describing is compared to something else. For example, when we say a semi-truck is big or a jumping spider is small, we are describing their size in relationship to ourselves. If we compared the semi-truck to an aircraft carrier, would we still describe it as being *big*? What about our friendly little jumping spider, if we compared her to a fruit fly, would we still describe her as being *small*? This is an expression of the principle of relativity.

Most of us do not appreciate the value and vulnerability of life, because we do not understand the scale of the universe we live in. We do not value life as we should, because it is seemingly everywhere. Life is in us, in the people around us, it springs from the dirt in the form of plants, and the oceans brim with living creatures of all shapes and sizes. However, when we change our rule of measurement from ourselves to the universe, we suddenly realize life is a tiny and isolated phenomenon of the material world. To give you an idea of just how small life is, consider how far away from us the sun is.

When you see the first rays of sunlight in the morning, it is easy to imagine the light you are seeing just left the sun seconds before it lit your bedroom. However, this is not the case. It takes light about eight minutes to travel from the sun to us. Light travels at roughly 186,000 miles per second, and there is 480 seconds in eight minutes. So how far has the light traveled to get here? It has traveled over 89,300,000 miles. If the sun were a big rock in the center of a shallow pond, and the earth were a lily pad, and we were crafty frogs, we would have to line up 3,572 lilies before we had a path that could take us from the shore to the big rock. Now, the measurements I used are rough estimates, but they are adequate to show how small life on earth really is.

If this is not enough to make you feel small, consider the earth is in a solar system, in a galaxy, in a universe so big we have yet to find the edge. To give you an idea of the size of the universe let us consider the Hubble Telescope. It is kind of a giant camera orbiting our earth above the atmosphere. As it goes around the earth, it takes pictures of space. Looking at these photographs one day, I became curious as to how big the objects in them were, and searched until I found the scale of the images I was seeing. To my absolute amazement, one of the photos I looked at was 256,000 light years across. This means if you traveled about 186,000 miles per second it would take you 256,000 years to travel from one side of the photo to the other.

To give you an idea of how big that is compared to the earth, let us return again to our path of lily pads. If the photo was a body of water, and we wanted to travel from one side to the other, how many of our earthy lily pads would we need to line up to do so? It would take 60,064,727,040,000 earth-sized lily pads to get from one side of the photo to the other. Also, remember this is just one photo of one tiny segment of space.

Now that we have a very faint idea of how big the universe is, do you know how many other planets have been found that could sustain life as we know it? As of yet, none have been found. So in light of this information I ask you, how valuable is life? Sure, life is all around us, but the whole of the earth is tiny in comparison to the universe, and life on earth is small compared to the size of our world. Two things make something valuable - how much of a demand there is for it in the market, and how much of it there is. Since we all need life in order to be here, I do not hesitate to say the demand for it is beyond measure. Once this demand is coupled with its rarity, then its value soars beyond calculation.

The only thing that rivals the worth of life is its fragility. Life is the most complex thing in the known universe, but it can be ended in a blink of an eye by fast moving lead, pointed sticks, or a lack of the elements it needs to survive. It is so fragile in fact, it cannot sustain itself, and in the end it breaks apart and turns again to dust. When you combine this fragility with how small it is in comparison to the space through which we move, we are like ants crossing an eight lane highway.

The principle of relativity shows us the scale of ourselves and our world. Knowing the scale of things also causes us to understand the value and vulnerability of the life we, and the beings around us, share. This inspires us to care for all living things, and the earth that sustains them. This would be reason enough to mention the principle of relativity, but it also teaches us something about the smallness of our problems.

Most of humanity gets wrapped up in the red tape of living, and the problems that come with being human. We lose our job and we think the world has ended, or our girlfriend leaves us and we lose the will to live. When we understand just how tiny and valuable life is, we realize how small and worthless the unpleasant things in life really are.

You lost your job? There are a million businesses all needing workers, don't throw away your rare life on account of that. Likewise, the loss of your lover is no big deal. Sure it hurts, and it seems too big to overcome, but that is just because we are measuring the event by ourselves and not realistically. There are millions of lovers needing love, but there is only one you. Do not let a tiny thing that can be replaced take your irreplaceable life.

These are just two examples of problems, but the principle applies to everything. What we eat, what we wear, who likes us, and who dislikes us does not compare to the wonder of being alive. Those who know their value, and how delicate life is, do not waste themselves. Neither, do they harm the living things around them, because they see their worth as well. Imagine if all knew and lived by this principle.

Seamlessness

When you listen to a beautiful symphony, and you hear the orchestra passionately playing, is there any note or silence the orchestra makes that is not a part of the song? Each note and rest blends and unites to make the entire piece resound with beauty. Likewise, when you make soap bubbles is there any gap in the surface? Not only are the bubbles gap-less, but if you touch one part of the bubble all of it will explode into nothingness.

As symphonies and bubbles are one, so is reality. There is not anything in the entire universe that does not affect the universe as a whole. Some things are like tossing a grain of sand into a lake. For a brief moment, a small ripple appears and then vanishes without disturbing much of anything. Then there are those things like a giant asteroid slamming into the ocean. They generate killer waves that can carry away mountains.

In reality, each thing is touching everything. This touching is not only a metaphor, it is a reality. My body is touching a molecule, which is touching a molecule, which is touching a space of emptiness, which is touching a molecule. This goes on and on until a line weaving through everything starts at my left hand and circles infinity to connect to my right. At all times, I am touching infinity and ride within its waves.

It is just like a spiders web; the entire web is woven in such a way that the outermost piece of silk is in constant connection with the center. All of us are centers and strings. Our consciousness is the central point of our web - our existence - that is moved and altered by events in the world around us. However, our life is also a string in the web of another that channels to them the happenings of the universe we both dwell in.

As a link in the webs of others, I can take actions that improve the quality of their home and life, or I can take actions that destroy them. We must be very aware of our actions due to the grand unity of all things lest we hurt or cause harm; just as we must be aware of the actions taking place around us for the same reason. By grasping this unity, we can better see the actual impact we are having upon reality, as well as the actual impact reality is having upon us.

Principles of the Internal World

Young Man had come a long way since he had first befriended Old Beauty. She had taught him much, and one day as he sat in a rice field watching the motions of the world, he suddenly realized though his eyes looked upon reality, sight happened in his mind. Young Man had become aware of his own consciousness, of the mini-verse within the universe, and he dashed to his to friend to share the news.

As he approached the door of the tent he paused, announced his presence, and waited to be admitted. Once inside he related to Old Beauty what he had experienced, and her face lit with joy. A glow came upon her and she said, "You have become aware of your mind my boy! Most are sleeping among the thoughts of others, letting the identities of others create their identity as well. However, you have found yourself, and now you can begin to finally seek the truth!"

Young Man was encouraged by his friend's approval, but the joy of his new breakthrough quickly was replaced by the solemn realization he knew nothing about the workings of his consciousness. Old Beauty watched these events transpire in his eyes, and before he could ask said, "Do not worry. If you know how to grow a flower, you know how to grow a mind. The principles governing the material world also govern the mental world. If reality is an ocean, then we are fish within it, and our consciousness is like our blood. As our blood is in constant motion, and changes its composition based on what we take into our bodies, so our mind is constantly being made or remade by our actions and the information we consume."

"Whatever we think or do in our minds, ripples throughout our consciousness, just as whatever we put in our blood alters our whole body. Mind is created by billions and billions of parts that need each other to survive. If any part fails there is disorder. Mind is not a ghost in the machine, but is the product of real machines that reproduce whatever you put into them. Just as the blood of each fish is made of what it has taken in from its environment, so is each individual consciousness unique and made from the information it takes in. There is no place in your mind not connected to the rest of it, so take care not to hide away poisons. If you do they will spread and sicken all that you are."

Chapter Ten

Now that we have looked at the external reality, we will turn our attention to the internal reality. It is of greatest importance to understand accurately how the mind works. Just as the dye in a pane of glass colors all the light that goes through it so will the presence of misunderstanding in our mind color every thought.

Human beings fail to keep themselves balanced. We like to have things in black and white, left or right, always or never, and our ways of thinking reflect this. The tragedy is this type of thinking prevents us from having a total understanding of life. Once a person has gained a love for one side they tend to dislike, ignore, or demonize the other side. However, the truth is each side is part of a greater whole, and the so called *differences* between the two sides arise from misunderstanding.

The above is also true of the inner and outer realities. Some philosophical and religious schools of thought want to make the search for truth a completely external quest. Feelings are ignored, if not totally disregarded, and inner exploration is forbidden because you might deceive yourself. These schools of thought put the entire experience of truth on the outside, and see all morality as being imposed onto them from an external code. To them human experience and intuition have little, if any, part to play in the search for truth and understanding.

Then, there are other schools who say the quest for truth something entirely internal. The outside world is taught to be a mental projection, a complex illusion, or so relative to each of us no one principle can apply to all humanity. In these systems, truth becomes a completely internal thing and there is no truth but one's own. To them, human experience and intuition is all that matters. The external world offers little to no insight into the nature of reality.

Between these two extremes, lies the middle path that also happens to be the right one. External reality exists apart from me and is not a creation of my mind. The external world is a tangible realm filled with real things governed by cosmic principles. This external reality and the truths about it came first then humanity was born into it.

Even though the external reality came first, it is not the only place where truth is found. It also lies within us. Feelings are not evil, they are windows into ourselves, and by knowing ourselves we better understand others and reality. Neither is self a horrible thing to be hated and beat. It is where my consciousness dwells, where my consciousness and life are made, and where I master love and forgiveness of others by learning to forgive and love myself.

The external reality and the powers it contains create mind, and mind in turn manipulates and creates the elements in the external reality. To understand the deepest truths of the universe, one has to understand both the inner and outer world. All we experience, all we sense, and all memory or thought happen exclusively inside our mind. Those who neglect the study of themselves will not understand anything else rightly; just as one who looks through a dirty window never sees the outside world as it is.

Understanding Inner Reality

A plant's life begins, is governed, and ends by the working of cosmic principles. The plant takes in water, light, and minerals from its immediate environment, and they become a part of it. Whatever chemical or mineral is taken into the plant through its leaves and roots becomes a part of the plant. They and the plant become one.

As a plant grows from the soil around it, so does the mental reality grow out of the physical world. All principles governing our minds - be they cosmic or cultural - are the same principles governing the segment of the material reality where we were born.

Mind is the flower, and our body and senses are like the roots and leaves. Our body takes in food, but our mind takes in the appearances, beliefs, and behaviors of the people around us. The ideas contained in the culture we were born into are set up inside of us as the measuring stick of reality. The way our people group lives life becomes the way life is supposed to be. The information we learn from our culture's authorities is the raw material used to create our inner world. This inner world can also be called our *learned reality*, because it is the view of reality our society has taught to us.

In the womb, our senses act like radio antenna capturing all the sights, sounds, smells, tastes, and textures of the world around us. These signals are transmitted to our mind where the data is interpreted and stored away for reference.

Waves of light from the external reality bounce off the material objects around us, giving us our sense of color, distance, shape, brightness, and pattern. Waves of sound made by the activities of external things pour into our ears allowing us to hear all the beautiful, and not so beautiful, sounds of life. The receptors covering our skin let us know the texture and temperature of objects in the external world. Microscopic chemical compounds entering our nose are interpreted by our brain and turned into scent. Meanwhile, substances brought into our mouth initiate chemical reactions interpreted in the mind as flavor. Through every pore and part of our body, reality is always pouring into us.

However, we are not allowed to freely experience this world and make our own conclusions about the things in it. We are taught what we should think, how we should feel, and what we should do in regards to every sensation entering our mind by the people around us. This complicates things greatly, and reveals one of the primary differences between the internal and external world.

The outside world, although it is influenced by our thought, is not created by our thoughts. However, the mental world is created exclusively by our thoughts. We not only sense things happening in the world around us, we attach ideas to them. Once attached, these ideas help us to determine if an experience or object is good, bad, true, false, funny, stupid, right, or wrong, and how we should interact with it.

Ideas are not taught to us as stand-alone things; we are made to learn entire systems of ideas. These gigantic systems act like the post office, and tell our brains where we should send each incoming stimulus. No matter what we are receiving from the outside world - color, sight, sound, smell, taste, ideas, pain - it is determined to be harmful, safe, good, bad, or any number of other values.

These values are determined not only by the thought system we have been programmed with, but are influenced by the data stored in our memory. For example, if I have had a bad experience with fried onions, even though my culture uses them frequently and generally thinks they are great, I will be inclined to dislike them. On the other hand, if I ate them and the event was a positive experience, the ideas of my culture and my own preferences will blend, and the onion will become extra pleasant in my mind.

After measuring an external object by our thought system, giving it meaning and value, our brain fires chemicals to generate emotions matching the meaning and value we have given it. If the thing is bad, dirty, or painful to us we have feelings of unrest, shame, impending doom, guilt or other negative mental events. If our mind informs us it is good, pure, or pleasant, then we get feelings of joy, peace, want, comfort, acceptance, or other positive sensations. These appraisals, and the emotional responses to them, spark ideas as well as prompting us to action. Receive input, appraise input, respond to input, and repeat. Moment by moment, day after day, until we die this cycle continues.

In the mind, there is not only the *actual sensation*, or what we physically sensed, we also couple to it a *belief sensation* - an emotion or perception added to the original stimulus by our mind. The belief sensation is the product of what actually is happening mixing with the ideas we have about it.

This brings us to another major difference between the external and internal world. In the external world, all the objects are real, but this is not the case internally. If a thousand people stood around a two ton rock, all viewers would be witnessing the same external object. Yet, each person would sense the rock in a different way. Each of us has different tools we are sensing the rock with, and different beliefs about the rock we are sensing. It does not matter if our ideas about the rock are wrong, if our mind believes them to be real, then it *is* real in our minds. What is true for the rock is true for everything in the external world.

To illustrate this, imagine two men walking through the woods who suddenly hear a sound. The sound emitted by an external source has been picked up by their ears and carried to their brains. Instantly, the two minds make an appraisal of the stimulus. One mind races through all it remembers and believes, determining it to be the call of a screech owl. This man is a woodsy sort, and has heard the owl speak on many occasions. However, the mind of the other man races through all it believes and remembers, determining the cry to be the scream of a man-eating mountain lion. He is unfamiliar with the sound, and the only data in his mind is a panther call he heard at the zoo.

The first man keeps walking calmly, while the second freezes in fear. The first tries to tell him it is just an owl, but the second knows - or more accurately believes - it is a killer beast, and will not be persuaded otherwise. Filled with fear, man two draws his weapon and empties into the night. Meanwhile the owl, seated in the branches well above the bullets, pauses to wonder at the rainless thunder and then cries again.

As with the voice of the owl, so it is with all things entering the human mind. Everything we sense has an actual source in the external world, but its substance is not half as important as what we believe it to be. No matter if it is a sight, sound, word, idea, smell, object, or creature most of us are unable to separate *actual reality* from *learned reality, actual sensation* from *belief sensation*. This is why few will ever know reality as it is.

Each and every creature on earth with a consciousness also has in their own mind a unique view of reality that cannot be fully understood by anyone else. The *inner reality* of each and every human, though we all come from the same reality and sense the same things, is very different because we each have different beliefs, memories, and sense tools.

These differences in perception and sensation cause us to think completely different about things in the external world. Even though you and I are standing in the exact same world, we are each living in different ones. There are about six billion people on planet earth, and each of them dwells in their own unique world despite them sharing the same cosmic address. Six billion inner realities are all perceiving and living in one external reality.

The human mind does not only have the ability to believe things, it also has the ability to imagine things. There is no limit to the visions, experiences, and ideas we can come up with in our minds. If one needs proof of this, all they need to do is look at the imaginary people and places contained in comic books, novels, movies, and video games. Humans can dream up anything.

Our imagination has played a key role in helping the human race solve giant problems and improve our reality. Yet, it has also played a key role in confusing our understanding of the world. If I get the idea in my head a pink elephant carries the world on its back, and each of us are the creations of a turtle wizard who lives in its ear, and I really believe this, in my mind reality actually works this way. Now, imagine I begin to give lectures, host television programs, write books, and devote myself to spreading the truth of the pink elephant around the world. This skews reality even further, because now I have persuaded millions of people to believe like me. Whenever an idea gains a following, the clockwork of culture begins to turn. After two of three generations, those who do not submit to the teachings of the ear wizard become social outcasts, doomed to wander the intestines of the pink elephant if they remain unbelievers.

In order to stop this phenomenon, we must strive with all our might to make our inner realities as much like the external reality as possible. We must toil with all our strength to separate *actual reality* from *taught reality*, and *actual sensations* from *sensations of belief.* This is the only way we can ever know the truth as it really is, and learn who we really are and our actual place in the universe.

From the time we were in the womb, we are exposed to the ideas, thoughts, and systems of those around us. These systems then become our norm, or the standard we appraise and evaluate everything by. It does not matter if the systems we are taught are correct in regards to the *external reality* - ac*tual reality* - because we believe them to be true. Our beliefs have been reinforced by our culture all our lives, so now the ideas of our society are the truths of our reality.

This is why I devote myself to truth and not to large organized religions or the sayings of some saint, sage, or guru. Religion has its place, but if the mind is only informed by one school of thought, it cannot think in any other way even if its own way of thinking is incomplete or incorrect. Not only this, but religions are so deeply bound to culture, emotion, and tradition it is hard to know what is true. One thing is certain, there is no way for every religious, philosophical, and spiritual system to be absolutely right. They can each be a little right and a little wrong, one can be right and all the others wrong, or all of them can be wrong. Yet, it is impossible for all to be absolutely correct.

We can only examine the thoughts, systems, and ideas filling the earth accurately, if we disattach our emotions from them and care only for the truth no matter what it is or where it may lead. If we do not disattach from our *learned reality*, we will never realize the *actual reality* correctly, or grow in our understanding of it.

Rather than letting books and people inform us about the universe, those who really want to know let the universe reveal itself. The seeker learns to separate actual from learned, true from believed, inner from outer, and then measures all by the objective standards of the cosmos.

This is the hardest thing anyone could ever do, but it is also the most rewarding. The quest to acquire truth is unending. We must tirelessly and fearlessly pursue it with a mind open to all information on earth, without any attachment to our personal understandings. If one fails to give equal and objective consideration to all points of view, how can they know what is true or false? Those who fail to do this are like the person who swears their basketball team is the best on earth, while refusing to look at the statistics or to play other teams.

As Without So Within

Having defined our inner reality, and learned something of how it is formed, we are going to look at how all the same principles governing the external reality also govern the inner reality. When one is lost upon the sea, and the compass they have been using has sinks to the bottom, they look up to the heavens and the stars guide them home.

As we sail further and further away from what we have been taught, our minds will reel, the waves will roll, and the compass will be lost. This is why we look to the principles of the universe that shine like stars in the night of understanding. As we do this, clarity will come, and a course to peace will open for our weary vessels.

Impermanence

This principle is as important and active in our mental world as it is in the physical. Few of us ever sit and think about how temporary our mental states are, and because of this we develop likes and dislikes, pulling and pushing us hither and thither. We are yanked and poked into doing things as we strive to maintain a state of mind we find pleasing, and avoid a state of mind we find distasteful.

All mental states and physical sensations are as temporary as the clouds passing over head. Anger, calm, expanded, dumb, happy, sad, wanted, unwanted, and all other states of mind come and go in a cosmic nanosecond. The wise learn this, and do not become overly concerned about obtaining pleasure or avoiding pain, choosing rather to pursue truth and the freedom it brings.

Each of us feel a unique set of emotions but everyone feels, so we all need to learn how to accept ourselves no matter what our current state of mind may be. When we have learned to accept our human emotions without letting them control us and admit our emotional needs, we have peace. We do not experience the self-loathing and emotional deprivation felt by those who make being human a crime.

The mind is a reactive device, submitting all kinds of ideas based on what it is thinking about and how it feels. These ideas range from good to sinister, and it is our consciousness that must pick what is best. So what does this have to do with the impermanence of the mental world? Many people mistake their thoughts and feelings with their choices and characters. When I feel attracted to a woman it is a natural part of being human, and is not evil in anyway. However, if I lie to get her sex this is not natural, and I would list it as a form of evil.

Likewise, if I am feeling bad, and the thought of ramming my car into the truck beside of me passes through my mind, I am not evil because this thought went through my head. It is just a stupid idea arising from the current attitude and focus of my reactive mind. Yet, if I choose to let my sorrow overtake me and ram my vehicle into the truck, I have shown my sorrow to be more important than my life and the lives of others. This is not best, and I would call it evil.

When we realize mind is the horse and consciousness the rider, we keep control even when our animal is tired, hungry, and feeling bad. We are not what we think and feel, and when we forget this we begin to push at the bad, pull at the good, and get mad when we cannot make them do what we want. Realizing all emotions are acceptable as long as they are rightly expressed, and all states are temporary, we do not become depressed when thoughts and feelings come, or depressed when they leave.

Another thing we must learn is time comes, goes, and has no mortal masters. I mention time because it is something humans made to express the changes we have been through, anticipate how much change we have yet to go through, and know what others are doing at any given moment. The natural world is the basis for time. Until we allow our minds to move naturally like the sun across the sky through the events of our lives, we will be subjected to a large amount of unneeded worry, fear, and want.

What has happened is no longer a part of our place in time it exists only as a memory. It is okay to use these memories as a dried flower to brighten our day, or as a book to better our understanding of how to act in the present. However, if we cling to our mistakes and our unpleasant experiences, they will only drag us down and keep us immersed in fear, shame, and suffering. If we cling to a broken past, its shattered bits will cut us until we let them go.

When we hold onto broken histories, not only do they cut us, but they cut those around us. We must remedy the unwise actions we have taken against others by seeking their forgiveness, and we must also forgive the harm done to us by others. As long as we carry the wrongs and mistakes acted out by us and against us at the forefront of our minds, we will be hurt daily by things done long ago. This pain will prevent total freedom and happiness from ever being ours.

Just as we need to let the past go, we must also let the future arrive moment by moment. Impermanence teaches us what has yet to happen will soon come to pass, and we need not fret about it, because it will soon be over. The future is built upon the present, and all we can do is make sure we understand and act with wisdom in this moment. As long as this is the case, the future will be wisdom. Whatever it is you want for your future live this moment in a way that will bring it to pass. The future is a flower blossoming from the seeds we plant today.

By realizing all experiences come and go, we are allowed to partake of joy without fearing its end, and feel sorrow without longing for its absence. When we realize now is the only time, we can free ourselves from the oppressing burdens of the past and become anything we wish to be.

How much pain do we cause ourselves by longing for what is gone and can never be again? How much blood has been shed to try to return a culture, or a race, to the *old ways*? If you wish to believe and behave like the ancients then do so, but do not rob those around you of the freedom to choose their own fate. Change is inherent in everything, and we either learn to move with the flow, or will be washed away and drowned by it. Adapt to every new moment, reevaluate every goal daily, and accept whatever comes and goes with grace. Do not waste your strength trying to retain what cannot be kept or prevent the inevitable, because you are going to need your strength to live.

Cause and Effect

In our mind, cause and effect are always in motion. When you feel a certain way, it is because a stimulus - be it image, idea, expectation, fear, or feeling - has entered your consciousness, and mind has reacted to it.

When I feel happiness, it is the product of what I am experiencing, and what I believe about the experience. My belief is more important than the event itself. The same goes for being sad. When I am gripped by sorrow it is because of what I have experienced, and how it measured up to my expectations. By understanding cause and effect, we can change every aspect of our mental world, and behave in ways that will cause us to get the most out of every moment.

There is no one on earth that is always joyous, and everyone will someday experience sorrow. Yet, if we always find ourselves in a cold and dark state of mind, then something is wrong. Sorrow and happiness lie inside of us, and we alone are responsible for their presence in our lives. Once we understand we are the only one responsible for our feelings, beliefs, and actions, we can guide them so they take us where we want to go, rather than being taken by them to places we do want to be.

The quality, content, and placement of my life in reality are my responsibilities. I cannot blame my conduct upon some evil force, nor can I attribute it to the ignorance of some divine being. It was I who weighed the options, made the choices, and took the actions that put me where I stand and made me what I am.

We cannot control circumstances, because of all the individual wills and factors involved in creating them. However, we can control our responses to them. I may have been abused in my past in any number of ways, but it is my choice to continue to suffer by dwelling there, or cause others to suffer by repeating the actions that hurt me. I may hate where I am in my life, but I am the one who is making the decisions keeping me there. Cause and effect is the key to all states of mind and body.

Just as the farmer will never reap a harvest she did not sow and cultivate properly, so we will never achieve a state of mind we did not take the proper steps to attain. Joy and sorrow are not the most important things in life, but the amount of them we possess is the product of choices we have made, beliefs we hold, and actions we have taken.

By filling our mind with right ideas about reality and self, and conducting ourselves in right ways, we enter into the deepest joys. It all rests upon the power of the will, and how we choose to use it. The health of our bodies and minds determine how healthy we are as individuals. Individuals combine to form societies, and societies combine to from human civilization. Thus, the health of the human world is determined by the actions each of us take as individuals, showing us yet another reason we should make our actions best.

Interdependence

Interdependence applies to the mind, just as it applies to reality. Each and every one of us has a massive system of thought we use to understand, evaluate, and react to the data entering our mind. The nature of a thought system is determined by how all of its parts work together, just like the biological, social, and ecological systems of the material world.

Each part of our thought system connects to and supports another part of it. In the material world stone, protein, heat, dirt, light, water, and animals form the building blocks of systems. However, in the mind, they are formed from ideas, information, memories, feelings, and beliefs.

To the simplest word, image, or idea in our memory, there is a network of ideas attached. Consider the word *green* for a moment, and just watch all the different images and ideas that flow into your mind. Colors, plants, places, people, flavors, events, attitudes - a sea of data floats into our mind as we recall all the things in our memory associated with the word *green*. Yet, this is only one word.

This interrelated mental framework is one of the reasons why it is so hard for us to open our minds to new things. We are afraid to open ourselves to the light of all knowledge, because we might find something we believe is wrong. This is undesirable because we like our habits and ideas and do not want to change them. We stay safely within the fence of what we know, so truth does not pop our comfort bubble.

However, the seeker for total understanding throws open the doors of mind to all information, all possibility, and considers everything in an unbiased way. It does not matter to them if they have to reject the ideas of close friends, loved family, ancient religions, or powerful nations; all that matters is truth.

Even though we want to protect ourselves from truth, the interdependence of mind requires us to ceaselessly improve our understanding. If a drop is poisonous enough to paralyze, what will a gallon do? If the foundation is built upon sand, how can the house stand? We must strive to prove all of our ideas true beyond any doubt, so our entire mind does not become corrupt and unsound.

Independent Nature

Even though every thought in our head is interconnected, they each have an identity of their own. Just like every whole in the universe is built up from small tangible individual pieces, so are the massive frameworks of the mental world.

As we grasp this concept, we will be able to analyze our minds and find inaccurate ideas. Once found, we can isolate the faulty thought, see what other thoughts in our mind are affected by it, and learn what we must do to fix the problem. We can grab hold of the bad ideas and throw them out, because the thoughts in our mind have substance.

Just as lead is bad due to the way its properties affect the body, so are certain thoughts bad due to the way their properties affect the mind. Just as one who eats mercury will be poisoned, so the one who feeds on ideas of worthlessness, hopelessness, fear, hate, and greed will be poisoned. On the other hand, those who consume ideas of virtue, hope, courage, and compassion will be energized and healthy, in the same way as one who has just eaten a fresh meal.

Those who deeply analyze themselves will quickly see what thoughts are inherently good, and what thoughts are inherently bad. Then they will be able to remove these thoughts, and by so doing awaken their mind and free it from guilt.

Many of the systems of thought in our world are not worth inviting into our minds as absolute guides to truth and life. However, we do not have to accept entire systems. We can select the true ideas and incorporate these into our lives, while leaving out the ideas that are untrue and hurtful. When one is devoted only to the truth, they take the truths a system contains and leave the errors. As they do this more and more, a system of pure truth begins to form. This does not mean the person has created their own philosophy, religion, or science. It means they are finding pieces of information that accurately describe reality, and applying them no matter who said them or where they came from.

Everything we sense and think is a mix of truth and illusion. It is the task of the sage to learn what truth is, how to find it, how to extract it from illusion, and then to go out and do it. It is like the bad spots of a banana. If we eat the bad spots - make them a part of us - then we will be made sick and start to suffer. However, if we cut out the bad spots, we can have a tasty treat to empower and refresh us. There are times when we have to throw out the whole banana, but even rotten bananas make great fertilizer. In our world, there is famine in the fields of truth, and wherever an edible morsel can be found one should not throw it away.

Do not let people trap you into defining your world in *all* or *nothing* terms. You will either starve because you see the bruises and think the whole system is spoiled, or you will swallow the whole thing and become ill. You can divide good from the bad, truth from dogma, and insight from superstition, just as you can pluck the leaves off of a tree, or remove bug bitten grapes from a cluster.

Actuality

Just as elements of the world have a definite existence outside of us, so do the thoughts in our mind have a definite existence inside of us. Thoughts alter our mood, change our actions, shape our world, and form the basis of our personality. Everything we think, whether it is true or not, alters our mind and world.

For example, consider a child who really believes - thanks to her big brother - a demon who likes to eat little girls is lurking in her closet, waiting to gobble her up the moment she gets out of bed. She buries herself in her covers and every sound, sight, or smell she perceives will be filtered through this powerful belief. Her mind will react as though the demon were really there. Her adrenalin pumps, her heart races, and she is gripped by fear. She *knows* the animated shadows are the movements of the monster, and fights sleep as though she were fighting for her life. However, mortality eventually overcomes fear, and exhausted she falls asleep.

When she wakes up the next morning she is amazed to be alive; few survive a night with a demon. When she told her brother how she barely made it out alive, he paused for a moment then asked if she was wearing red. Quietly she said she had been wearing her favorite red socks and her brother informed her that must be the reason for her survival. Demons do not like red.

The little girl was excited to hear this news, but her joy gradually gave way to horror as she realized she only had one pair of red socks. Thinking deeply, she decided to talk mother into buying her six more pairs of red socks with the money in her piggy bank. Running to mommy with piggy in hand, she pleaded to be taken to the retail store. This puzzled her mother, who asked the young lady why she wanted to go so badly. As the little girl answered, slowly the plot was revealed, and her mom - after relieving the child of her fear - went off to put some fear into her brother.

Just as the little girl's beliefs affected her reality, so do our beliefs affect ours. All ideas we hold true alter our mental chemistry and our worldview - no matter if they are ideas of truth, love, hate, kindness, religion, science, or aliens. Even if our thoughts do not have any basis in reality, they are still real to us. Through us they enter into the real world and change it, and in this way the real is shaped by illusions.

For this reason, we must make sure not to merely trust a thing to be true, rather we must test it until we know it is true. Since our thoughts shape our reality, we cannot afford to let illusions live in us. Otherwise, we will live in a world of lies and spread lies throughout the world.

If something has the ability to alter me, the world, and the people around me it is real, even if it does not have weight, color, texture, flavor, or smell. My consciousness is created by the processes of my brain and body, but it is not in my body. If you cut open my head, you will find the brain that creates my mind, but my consciousness will not be inside. Just as consciousness is real without having substance, so are thoughts real. They form the basis of all human experience and build cultures as blocks build houses.

Thoughts are energy just like everything else in existence. If I pick up a book, its binding, the pages, and the ink upon them are all made of matter, which is itself made of energy. If I open the book and begin to read the words, my mind takes in the words through my eyes, and decodes the symbols. This entire process is a chain of chemical and electric reactions. Consciousness commands the brain, and the brain sends millions of bio-electric signals telling the body to find the book, open the book, and look at the book. Consciousness then commands the brain again, and a million more signals are sent that directs awareness to read the words, decipher the words, and to consider their meaning.

This process also happens in reverse when a book is being made. The consciousness of the writer uses biochemical commands to make his body write symbols expressing the content of his mind. Thus, thought - beginning in the form of electrochemical signals inside the mind - is changed into symbols made of atomic energy. After this, it ventures out into the world in the form of a book. Then, another mind commands her will to move her body through the material world, gain possession of the book, and then convert the atomic energies back into electrochemical signals, releasing the author's meaning inside her mind.

All of this is one massive energy exchange, revealing ideas exist in our mind as thoughts, but in our brains as chemical compounds and electrical charges. These bio-electrical processes can be measured and manipulated by our inner consciousness, or by elements of the external world.

Ideas affect everything. They are not intangible they are real and powerful mental objects. It does not matter if they lack substance they still instantly affect the material parts of ourselves, and then through us enter and alter reality. Because of this we should never forget our thoughts create us and our world. Thought is a mental substance, building upon itself to make consciousness, just as protein and minerals make the body. If you take in bad thoughts they will create bad feelings and bad realities. Therefore, observe your thoughts lest you make yourself sick and your reality suffering.

Replication

Just as like flows from like in the material world, so does like flow from like in the mental world. Many of us plant negative ideas, dark futures, and hopelessness in the soil of mind, and then wonder why we have a garden of despair. We have learned how the realness of thought changes us, but we must also learn what we sow in our mind is what we will eat.

We cannot plant divisive ideas in ourselves, because then division will rule our minds. Then, as we express our minds we shape our world. If we plant anger, we should not wonder why we never eat the fruit of peace. We cannot sow corruption, delight in cravings, and then expect to harvest purity and self-control.

What we put into our mind is what our mind puts into our life. What we consume mentally is what we become mentally. By understanding this, we come to realize the power to be what we want to be resides within ourselves. How do we do this? By seeking out and mentally consuming those things we wish to have. Just as eating brings the protein into the body that is used to make its parts, so does mind build itself from the sights, sounds, and information taken in from its environment.

In light of this, is it any surprise those who immerse themselves in the Bible become devout Christians, while those who read only atheistic works become atheists? Is it any wonder those who often consider the words of Buddha become Buddhists, or those who delight in the ideas of Hitler become fascists? Neither does the information we take in have to be real in order to change our mind. Those who dine upon romance become hopeless romantics, while those who feast upon silly humor become silly comics. This cycle is at work in every system of thought be it sacred, material, fake, real, or otherwise. Our mental disposition seeks like minds and in turn their ideas strengthen our preexisting attitudes and deepen our attachment to a way of thinking.

Once we understand fully how thoughts influence everything, we suddenly realize the tremendous responsibility we have to everyone to make sure we are thinking rightly. We not only need to seek out and consume good things, we also need to make sure the things we consume are true in the highest sense, and not just educated idiocy or inspirational illusions.

The outside world is the result of our thoughts and desires, the inner world is the result of what we have chosen to take in, and what we put into the world is what we get back. When our lives fall apart it is not the working of fate or an act of some supernatural force, it is due to our own actions, thoughts, and choices.

If I seek beauty in the world around me I will find it, and if I seek ugly things I will find those as well. This is because the earth is filled with good and bad. My mind is only being attracted to the ideas and experiences it has a taste for. The good and bad experiences we have are being invited into our lives by our habits of thought and action. What you are doing is simply coming back to you.

Once something I enjoy has been introduced into my life, I start to seek it. As I seek it my actions are changed, and as I experience the object of my desire, I want it even more. This causes me to like it more, liking it more I seek it more, and consuming it more frequently causes me to more closely reflect its attributes.

As this cycle becomes habit, I surround myself with people who think and enjoy the same things as me. Then together we repeat the cycle, further reinforcing in us the habits and ideas we share. However, groups are composed of many people, and since every person has many unique thoughts, I am introduced to new ideas I either accept or reject. If I accept these new ideas, I am taken into yet another group of people where I am exposed to even more new ideas and the cycles roll on.

In this way, people groups end up creating the personality and lives of those within them. What I choose to invite into my mind will make me like it is, and in turn my influence will make others like me. When people stay in a group, and refuse to consider any idea not in their group, they are insulated from all ideas and information on the outside. In this way, groups who claim to have ultimate truth and encourage separation from others, slowly conform the unaware by means of repetition, shame, guilt, fear, and ignorance.

In the end, the individual is indoctrinated so deeply self is lost, and only finds meaning when it is a part of the collective. Know how groups eat away at individuality, know how your mind works, and above all strive to obtain the truth. Once obtained, do not let peer pressure force you to conform to ideas that are illogical and limiting.

Most of us have really messed up our lives, but this principle gives us hope. No matter what we are, or what our people group has made us, we can become something different by educating ourselves, and exposing our minds to all wisdom and knowledge. Once we change our mental diet and daily practices, our new ideas begin to change all we are. Then, the mechanisms of mind will begin to reshape us yet again. If our actions, thoughts, and words are right, then we will daily improve ourselves and the world around us.

One caution however, even though the principle is indeed that easy, when you are changing the actual habits it is hard. When you ingest a principle and act according to it, your physical body develops cravings, remembers pleasures, attaches experiences, and learns to dislike the absence of the objects you desire. If you think you can indulge in a chaotic and destructive cycle and just jump out at any time you may find your feet do not wish to move. However, do not fear. The power to change the darkest of nights into the brightest of day is inherent in the powers of beauty, compassion, peace, truth, joy, hope, and wisdom. By feeding upon these, you will be stronger than a million vile habits and never without courage.

Relativity

The principle of relativity is at work in the inner reality more than it is in the external reality. Human beings are limited in how much they can sense, and their minds reflect these limits. What I have not sensed I cannot know. All I can ever know is limited by the amount of time I have spent acquiring knowledge, as well as the type and quality of the tools I used to collect it.

For example, in my past I was sincerely religious and judged all the people I met by the ideas and experiences stored in my mind. Thus, whenever I saw somebody doing something I felt was evil, I assumed they had the same body of knowledge as me. I would label them as evil and set about correcting them. In this way, I proved myself to be totally ignorant about the principle of relativity.

Just as the place I am standing determines my view of the world, so the place of my birth determines my view of life. Each and every human has an understanding of things that is one of kind. Each of us have started in different places, encountered different obstacles, and received different information. When two people come from the same culture, they see things from a similar point of view, because they started in similar places. However, even identical twins, born and raised in the same house, have their own experience of reality. No one else on earth can ever think, feel, or be exactly like any other person.

Not only do we have individual ideas and memories, we also have our own personal set of tools we explore reality with. My eyes see things differently, my ears hear things differently, my tongue tastes things differently, my skin feel things differently, my nose smells things differently, and certainly my mind processes things differently than everyone else on the face of the earth. All of our senses work in similar ways, but the information they collect is different to varying degrees. Some people have excellent hearing and some are born blind, some can smell the faintest of scents while some cannot feel pain. Though we each share a common reality, we experience it in ways no other human ever has or ever will.

The differences in us arising from the different ideas about reality in our cultures are *learned differences*. Those differences in us rising out of our unique way of sensing and experiencing reality are called *mechanical differences*. Due to these differences, none of us have any right to comment on the behavior or understanding of those around us until we understand them. Even then, if we do not possess wisdom and a genuine concern for their well-being, we should just keep our mouth shut.

Whenever we pass judgment, or make a moral evaluation of others without a full knowledge of the relativity built into human experience, we are only going to do harm. The person before us may be the most irresponsible, selfish, and unpleasant person on earth to be around, but we should never criticize or condemn them. We do not know their history or their thoughts. They could have been abused as children, betrayed as adults, or suffered some horribly traumatic event.

Even though these things do not justify their behavior, what if they never had access to the philosophical or spiritual ideas that have bettered you? If this is the case, then you become the representative of the knowledge and wisdom they need to be whole and happy humans. How selfish it would be to remove from them this possibility by rejecting them, because you do not like the way they look, think, or behave.

Not only do we judge others of our kind by our personal standards, we also judge the natural world by them. We call the processes of nature that interrupt or destroy human life *bad,* and relate to them as we would to a person. At times, we go so far as to attribute the purely physical and mechanistic process of life to supernatural spirits who wish us harm or health.

We also project human understandings and morals onto the animal kingdom. Cute and non-threatening things we see as being innocent and sweet, while ugly and life threatening things we see as being evil and destructive. However, in reality we are merely justifying our violence against what reminds us we are not the most powerful or intelligent beings on earth.

When a female cheetah kills a gazelle's fawn, or a lioness kills the calf of a water buffalo, we somehow feel an injustice has been done. However, if we would look at the whole life of these big cats, rather than only when they are in the role of predator, we would watch these mothers take the meat back to their young so they can live. How blind we are to ourselves - do we not see how humans kill and eat more animals than any other thing on earth? Sometimes doing so only because we want to feel the thrill of the kill? If any are to be judged by the principles of another, we should be judged by the members of the animal kingdom. They use what they need, waste little, and live in a way not harmful to their world.

The life of a bat is known only unto the bat living it. Other bats may have a little better idea, but all other forms of life can only watch how the bat works and imagine what it must be like to be it. As with bats so it is with people. We cannot afford to imagine the histories and thoughts of those around us we must communicate with one another so we can understand the common humanity we share. The desire for happiness, well-being, and the opportunity to provide for those we love is common to all.

Perhaps the most important aspect of relativity pertains to a personal understanding of truth. We each have an idea of what is possible and what is impossible, what is truth and what is error. However, our ideas come from our culture and our teachers, and could very well be wrong as much as they are right. Not only do we each have a unique type of knowledge, we also have a unique type of ignorance.

Our level of understanding is the only limit to our potential. Just as a group of sparrows thought the idea of a bird flying from one side of the world to the other was ridiculous, the geese knew better. By learning to see things from other perspectives, we also learn to see the limits of our own understanding. When we strive diligently to expand our wisdom and knowledge, we are empowering ourselves to burst the confines of our petty expectations, and leap over the walls of our uninformed imaginings. Those who can see things from every imaginable angle, and realize there are angles they cannot imagine, have gotten beyond the walls dividing us. They are entering into the very substance of reality.

Seamlessness

As all things in the material world associate with and affect every other things in reality, so it is in the minds of conscious beings. Every thought and idea you and I have about anything mingles together inside our mind. To accept any idea or to reject any idea affects everything.

Trivial concepts that do not play a big role in our life float into and out of our minds, but even these can become major if we focus on and attach to them. This is why we need to let the trivial things be trivial, so they do not swell up and alter the entire course of our thoughts and lives.

Even though my view of reality may not accurately reflect the real world, my understanding still constantly touches and shapes reality. There is no separation between mind and matter. Mind is made possible by the brain, brain is connected to the body through millions of nerves, and body is in constant contact with the external reality through millions of sensory devices. There is no division between the internal and the external reality, even when my ideas about the world are totally wrong.

This total seamlessness is yet another reason to pursue an absolutely accurate view of reality with all our strength. If my view of life is false, but I behave as if it were real, I draw others into false habits and wrong understandings.

If we desire constant improvement and well being for all, we must take time to improve and heal ourselves, and not get lost in living. There is nothing wrong with enjoying life, but if we devote ourselves to pleasures, our delight will become our master, and our existence slavery. By seeking wisdom we gain power, and by power we can live a pleasurable and victorious life.

By seeking we find wisdom, by wisdom we learn of the external world, and by learning about the external world we come to understand ourselves. Learning about ourselves we know how to rebuild our lives, construct our future, and see the boundless undivided infinity containing it all.

Universal Flow and the Moral World

Young Man knew how hard Old Beauty worked to find and prepare her meals, so he decided to bring her a surprise breakfast. Waking with the chickens, he cooked the perfect morning dish to perfection, and trekked to the Mountain's top to deliver his gift. As he approached, he heard Old Beauty singing an unfamiliar tune. Straining his ears, he could make out the words of a one stanza song, "Nameless way, Heaven's way, walked by young and old; making everything, and revealed by all that's made."

"What are you singing?" he said suddenly. Young Man had forgotten Old Beauty did not know he was there, and for his crime he caught a stick of fire wood with his face. Realizing who it was by the groans that followed, Old Beauty said with a grin in her voice, "You would think by now you would have learned not to surprise an old woman?" Still holding his nose, he lifted the sack of food in his other hand, and mumbled through the fingers holding his nose about his kind intentions. Apologizing for the wound and expressing her gratitude for his kind gesture, Old Beauty gathered the dishes needed for their meal, and they sat down to eat.

While they were eating, Young Man asked, "What were you singing about?" Old Beauty responded, "Have you never heard of the Way?" Her tone was thick with curiosity as she continued, "How can this be?" Young Man replied, "Though I am young I am not unlearned, yet I have not once encountered a thing by this name? I...", before he could finish his thought Old Beauty sparked, "The Way is not a thing!" Realizing how important it was to her by her abrupt reaction, and not wanting to inadvertently catch another stick of wood, the young man asked, "What then is the Way?" Old Beauty's scowl broke into a trance-like stare accompanied by a spunky smile, and she said, "If I tell you what the Way is I have already misrepresented it, for limited expressions can never express what is without limit. Yet, if I say nothing you will never be able to walk it, so knowing Heaven will forgive my necessary clouding, I will try to put it simply."

Old Beauty's eyes lit and she said, "The Way is truth, the way is like a tree. It is undivided though capable of being divided into innumerable parts. If a thousand people looked at it from a thousand angles, they would each see a lot of it and a lot of it would be hidden from each of them. Every part of it is the same as every other part, or different depending on what the viewer chooses as the rule of measurement. Leaves are like roots because they both bring in nutrients, but if we compare them based on their appearance they are very different. The way is visible and invisible, yet both of its parts behave in the same way."

"For every action it takes that can be seen, there is an equal and opposite reaction that cannot be seen. For every action it takes that cannot be seen, there is an equal and opposite reaction that can be seen. This is like the tree's top and the tree's bottom. As the branches move up into heaven before our eyes, the roots dig down into the earth where we cannot see, and as limbs have many leaves, the roots have many fingers. One side loves the light, and the other loves the dark, yet there are no paradoxes anywhere to be found in trees. Likewise, the only paradoxes in the way are created by lack of knowledge in the viewer."

"The manner in which the tree lives and climbs to heaven, is the same manner in which the ant lives and climbs the tree. In this is shown how the same way is walked by all things, yet all things walk it according to their nature and capacities. Those who cooperate with the way create sweetness and goodness, just as farmers cooperate with the tree to make fruit. Those who neglect the way shrivel and rot like fruit on a neglected tree. The way is simple enough for a child to enjoy, and deep enough to entrance the wisest of minds - just as children can play in a pine's branches, yet biologists and wise men can lose themselves in its lessons and complexities."

"The way is Heaven's purest expression of itself. Without end, without beginning, it shows us all perspectives and their limits, all truths and their connections, and no one will ever know it fully. Watch heaven, observe earth, learn from all fools, and question all sages, and you will come to know the way. If you do not now understand do not worry, it is deep, and none can fully fathom it in a hundred lifetimes. I do not expect you to grasp it in a moment."

Chapter Eleven

With a basic understanding of what reality and consciousness are, how they work, and how they relate to one another, we can now look at one of my favorite aspects of reality - the flow of the Universe. This giant cosmic motion is the flow made from the individual motions of all things, just as the flow of a river is made by the movement of all the individual drops of water in it. This motion is not a principle inside of reality it is the motion producing reality itself.

In order to understand reality, it is necessary to break it down into smaller parts. Can you imagine learning all the principles of mathematics at once? Numbers, addition, subtraction, division, multiplication, algebra, calculus, geometry, and all the rest being poured into you on your first day of kindergarten? Do you think you could understand it? If you think that is a lot to be told at one time, imagine sitting in a room with twenty master scholars from all the fields of human knowledge teaching you all they know at once. All hope of learning anything would be lost. As an ant hill is made grain by grain so our understanding improves piece by piece and level by level.

However, there is a problem built into this necessary division of reality - we end up getting the idea it is truly divided, and never put all the parts back together. This is a real problem in our day and age. We have categorized, divided, labeled, and split so much we live in a universe resembling more of a jigsaw puzzle than it does a functional reality.

It would be bad enough if only our world was segmented, but as we have learned everything affects everything. These divisions of understanding have also fragmented our lives. We have a million different boxes we put ourselves in and running back and forth between them exhaust us and ruins peace of mind. Until we restore the undivided oneness of reality we will not have peace, because our minds will remain divided against themselves.

The way to peace and wealth in life is only found by harmonizing ourselves with the natural flow of the universe. This harmony begins by observing in spite of all its parts, reality moves as a unified whole we are a part of. External reality, internal reality, and the principles we have looked at are all individual currents running through the universe, yet they all converge into one grand flow.

This means we cannot harmonize ourselves with one principle while neglecting another, and expect our lives will move in harmony with the stream. We must harmonize with every truth we know, or we will be like the salmon who fight against the current to reach the rivers head. Even though they may reach their goal, they are wasted and their accomplishment becomes their grave.

The presence of each conscious and unconscious part of this universe exerts an influence on the whole that cannot be stopped. It does not matter if these parts are moving or still, just by occupying a place in space and time they affect it. The sort of influence each part has is determined by the internal structure of that particular part. Stars give light due to their construction, birds give songs, plants give oxygen, cows give milk, and humanity produces insight or insanity.

Barring the majority of humans, all parts of reality work in flawless harmony with one another. Each and every action taken by one thing causes another action to take place in response to it, and this in turn creates another action. This chain of action is what creates our reality, and the ability we have to conceive it.

To make sense of this, we can imagine reality as a giant human being. The giant has many parts inside of it that all seem to be doing their own thing: the lungs breathe, the heart pumps, the stomach churns, and the mind directs. However, each part affects every other part in the body. The heart contracts and blood moves out, as the blood moves it carries nutrients through the arteries, as these nutrients move cells are nourished. The nourishment gives the cells energy, the energy enables them to do work, and the work grants us being and consciousness.

If conscious life is the flow of the body, reality is the flow of the universe. Even though all the parts of reality seem to be doing different things, they are actually moving as one motion. Each part contributes something to the others, and the simultaneous actions produce us and the reality we live in.

Each piece has its part to play in this eternal flow, vibrating like a cosmic symphony. Each part is like an instrument made in its own special way, functioning in its own special way, and producing its own unique sound. We must carefully learn how each part of everything works so our instrument - our life - plays in harmony with the music of the universe.

The symphony is not the product of any one instrument, but the more instruments play, the clearer the song becomes. By consuming this infinite melody, we can experience the boundless totality words cannot express due to their inherent limits.

A Principle of Principles

There is always perfect balance in the material universe. For every give there is a take, for every part of energy there is a place of emptiness and everywhere light is there is shadow. Everything in the universe strives for perfect equilibrium and despises disharmony.

This striving for balance is the dynamo driving the primordial flow of the universe. If all things were to finally succeed in reaching total balance, the universe would grind to a halt, and life would come to an end. Every process we see is being created through the use of energy. When a dog runs, it is turning the organic-compounds it has eaten into electrochemical energies that fuel and direct motion, as well as into proteins which form the parts being moved. While the dog lives there is imbalance. It uses the energy it has and so depletes it, this creates a need for energy causing the dog to hunger. When it eats, balance is returned, and the process goes on. The only time there is permanent balance is when the creature is dead.

The processes of the material world are also products of forces striving for harmony with each other. The wind is the movement of air from one side of the earth to the other, as the opposite side is heated by the sun. The water cycle is made by heat the sun produces as the elements in it are fused together; available energy being turned into working energy producing the light and warmth earth enjoys. When all of the unstable fuel has given off all of its energy and attained balance with the world outside, the sun dies and with its passing so would life on earth.

If things continue as they are and time goes on long enough, all things will run out of energy - a state of cold balance that has come to be known as *entropy*. However, even though the motions of larger things and beings are driven by imbalance, without the delicate balance of the atom nothing in the universe would exists.

Each atom has at its center a positively charged speck of energy, called a proton, and most have a speck of energy having neither a positive or negative charge, called a neutron. The positive charge of the proton keeps another particle of energy, called an electron, in orbit around it. It is the number of electrons each atom has that determines what element it is. If the attractive force between the protons and electrons are too weak they will fly out of orbit. Likewise, if the force is too great the electrons will be pulled into its center. If either of these were the case, energy would not form atoms, atoms would not form elements, elements would not form matter, and since everything is made from matter, the universe as we know it would not exist.

This simultaneous need for balance and imbalance, set against the back drop of the total unity of the universe, makes a wonderful introduction to the principle of *Ebb and Flow*. All parts of the expansive cosmic ocean are made from differing energies, all behaving as a type of ebb or flow. Balance and imbalance, light and dark, hot and cold, positive and negative, masculine and feminine, strong and weak, fill and drain, somethingness and nothingness, internal and external, motion and stillness, are all examples of the interplay between active and passive forces. This rest in unrest, these contrasting natural forces always striving for harmony, is inherent in all things. This interchange and harmony was witnessed by the sages of ancient China, who created a visual parable of the interplay between ebb and flow called the yin-yang.

Harmonious or Inharmonious Action

The yin-yang is a sorely misunderstood symbol. As is the case with most things, people never look into its meaning. Many I talk to think it symbolizes a little good in all evil and a little evil in all good, but this is not the case. The yin-yang is a metaphor for the working of everything in reality, and even though it can teach us valuable lessons about the quality of one's actions, it is not a moral illustration. There is balance and harmony among all things in the natural world, except in the realm of human thought and action.

If one is not careful, they will confuse the metaphors used to describe the internal and external realities with those realities themselves. Whenever we do this, it leads to a false understanding of what reality is and how it works. In the area of *right* and *wrong* this is definitely the case. The metaphor of light and darkness is one of the primary examples used to describe the energies of good and evil. Yet, it does not express the reality of good and evil, because no limited expression can totally express an unlimited reality.

Evil is not darkness, night, or blindness. Evil is wrong thinking flowing from one mind to another blinding perception, inflaming selfishness, creating unwise actions, and multiplying in the presence of ignorance. Likewise, good is not light, day, or sight. Good is correct thinking flowing from mind to mind eradicating illusion, evaporating selfishness, creating wise action, and multiplying in the presence of humility.

This is just one example used to describe good and evil, but it is sufficient to demonstrate the problem of confusing the reality with representations of it. Wherever there is light there will always be darkness, but this does not apply to good and evil. In order for one to smile, laugh, and be at peace must they also frown, cry, and be filled with chaos? In order for a woman to enjoy intimacy with her new groom, must she first be raped by a stranger? In order for a man to have and love his son, must he first hate and murder a daughter? The answer to all of these is obviously no. It is perfectly possible to have the best things in life without having any of the bad. Unfortunately, we have good and bad on earth. However, we could have only the bad so there is still reason to be joyful.

Good and evil are two hidden currents running through the ocean of reality. These currents are themselves invisible even though the words, thoughts, and actions they produce are not. These are the powers driving and governing the minds of every human being, to a greater or lesser degree.

When I speak of good, I mean the energies which give rise to all purity, truth, and wisdom; the ennobling energy contained in all the knowledge and expressions of humanity. I do not speak here of social norms, cultural standards, or personal preferences, but of right action and right thought.

When I speak of evil, I mean the energies which give rise to corruption, falsehood, and ignorance; the debasing energy contained in all the knowledge and expressions of humanity. I am not talking about a regional norm, imposed personal standards, or social taboos, but rather wrong action and wrong thought.

It is true right and wrong can exist in the same system, book, or culture. Yet, even when they co-inhabit they do not mingle, just like iron does not mix with clay. They are forever independent of each other. Right and wrong thinking does not mix, and the minds of those who try to keep both types of thought and action will only prevent themselves from realizing their potential and experiencing peace. Wrong actions are actions that do not harmonize with the nature of reality and its natural flow. It is the mental and metaphysical equivalent of sticking your tongue in a light socket.

It is true the right and wrong actions I take can produce outcomes opposite their nature - bad leading to good or good leading to bad. However, this is only because goodness has called forth indignation from evil minds, or evil has moved pure minds to compassion. Not only this, but being a life form limited in power, duration, and understanding there is only a limited amount of good I can do.

For example, if I give my money to a cause close to my heart, another cause does not get my money. This does not mean I have done good and evil, it just means I did all the good I could do with what I had available to me. This applies to any act of goodness a human might do. Furthermore, merely because my right thinking reveals the wrong thinking of another, and they commit wrong acts because of it, the goodness of my action is not nullified. Neither is my goodness responsible for their evil. My good and their evil are individual actions taken by individual wills, due to the thoughts in our individual minds.

Good and evil have more to do with the motives and intelligence of the mind doing them, than they do with specific deeds. When one has done they best they can, even if the outcome hurts themselves and others, if they have done so through ignorance they are not guilty of committing pure evil. They still must take responsibility for their actions, there will still be harmful consequences, and once they are cured of ignorance they should set about making amends for the harm they have caused. Yet, since their intention was not impure, and they did not have full understanding, they should not taste the full power of justice.

As we discuss what good and evil really are, it is beyond important we remember the role understanding and motive have to play in each of them. If we forget that intention is more important than external conduct and appearance, we will misunderstand everything, and in the end see vice as virtue and virtue as vice. It is all about will, its intent, and how much the person understands about themselves and the reality they live in.

How Are We to Measure Good and Evil

If good and evil are to be found, pursued, or avoided, how are we to know what is pure and what is corrupt if goodness and evil are terms describing what the mind is thinking? How can we judge the morality of others when the things we are trying to evaluate are invisible, and we cannot read their mind?

In order to determine if an action, idea, or thing is right or wrong, there are several things we must do. The first is to understand the thing or being we are evaluating in its natural context. This means I cannot pick an idea or person of another culture, and evaluate them with my culture's ideas of good and evil. Instead, I need to understand the entire social, religious, and personal influences that have affected what I am evaluating. Then, I must see if the effects of what I am evaluating contribute to the betterment or harm of all.

Something else we must consider when deciding if an action is good or evil, is to determine the level of understanding the doer of the deed has. If I know something is going to hurt and destroy and I do it anyway it is pure wrong action, and all the weight of justice can justly fall on me. However, if I do not know something to be right or wrong, how can anyone make a moral judgment about my actions? Someone may be able to know if my action is harmful or helpful, but whether I am good or evil they cannot judge.

It is very hard to know if another is good or evil, because we are ignorant of their experiences, motives, and mental health. It is easy to know if an action is constructive or destructive, but if we want to know whether the mind of another is good or evil, we have to wait until their words and actions express clearly the nature of their mind. Even then it can be difficult. Because of the difficulty involved in knowing the minds of others, the wise do not spend their time judging and weighing the actions and lives of others. Rather, they spend it studying their self, determining right, and seeking harmony with the universal flow.

However, the most important aspect of understanding good and evil is to get beyond the understanding of good and evil we already have. The concepts of good and evil are universal. Yet, what good and evil are is defined differently by almost every religion on earth. Therefore, to grasp what good and evil really are, we have to get beyond the names our culture has applied to certain ideas and actions, and into the substances behind the names. We have to get out of the conceptual world, and into the real world.

Beyond Good and Evil

One fall, Young Man and Old Beauty were seated on an overlook on one side of the Mountain. There they were watching the harvesters collect the grain produced by the hard work they done throughout the year. Just then, Young Man caught sight of a group of vultures passing over the field. All his life he had been told the vulture played a part in the introduction of evil into the world. As he watched the vultures fly, he became so disgusted by the sight of the wretched bird he could not help but growl quietly, "Evil beast." Old Beauty heard this; her hearing was better than her companion gave her credit for, and she asked, "What about that beast makes it evil?"

Young Man was puzzled because he thought everyone knew the evil of the vulture. In fact, it was such common knowledge he had never thought about it. Embarrassed by his lack of thought, Young Man supposed he would cover it up by casting the question back onto his friend, and in the most scholarly tone he could produce retorted, "Why do you think it is not evil?" At this point you would think Young Man would have known better than to challenge Old Beauty in such a way, but his new found understanding of things seemed to interfere with his memory.

Old Beauty, looking through his shallow attempt replied, "If you insist on trying to hide your shallowness of thought then allow me to reveal it for you. The reason I do not think the bird is evil is because I only look at the bird, and you look at the bird through the stories you have been told about it. The bird is just a poor beast, it knows nothing of good or evil, it only follows the dictates of its nature. Long ago its ancestors acquired a taste for dead things, the more they ate dead things, the more they liked them. Eventually, their natures become inclined to dead flesh, and their bodies adapted to eating it."

"The smell of rotten flesh to the vulture is as the smell of roses to us, but measuring it by ourselves we call it vile. The role models of the vulture taught it day and night dead flesh was best, and the best ways to eat it. Yet, again we measure its actions by the things our role models taught us and call it filthy. The poor creature does us a great service by removing the dead things from our land, and ensures no lost life is wasted, yet we spurn it and label it a tool of demons. A beast that doesn't even have the capacity to know the meaning of evil, is forced to bear the title by creatures that should be smart enough to know good and evil only exist in their minds."

"Only humans are wise enough to know the nature of good and evil. Only they have the capacity to recognize these things, and to them alone does the choice between good or evil present itself. Even though good and evil exist in the ultimate sense, most never understand them truly. Most accept whatever definitions their *teachers give, and in this way good has come to be called evil and evil good by the people of our time."*

"Evil does not exist as a substance in the external world. If it did then Heaven could be charged with its creation. Evil exists only in the minds of humans, and by choosing to indulge in it they brought, and still bring, it into the world. Thus, we are responsible for all the death and suffering evil causes. The evil mind sees evil everywhere, seeks evil at all times, pours forth evil every moment, and then weeps for the evil in the world. They are ignorant that they are the source of the world's despair. Because I am free of social conventions and petty traditions I know the vulture is not evil, and because you are still filled with both, you believe it is."

Chapter Twelve

The natural world, what has not been created or affected by the human mind, exists in a totally neutral moral state. Elements, plants, animals, bacteria, viruses, and everything else in the universe is neither good nor evil. In fact, in the material world good and evil do not exist. They are not tangible substances like gold or silver, they are mental substances, and exist only in the human mind. Wherever morality is seen or experienced outside of our minds, it is only because the mind of another human has altered an element of reality.

To demonstrate the natural world's lack of evil, imagine a person walking through the woods startles a snake and is bitten by it. Did the snake commit an evil deed? The snake is just trying to protect itself. Again, let us say you get a horrible virus causing you to cough, vomit, and run a fever. Is the virus evil? It is unpleasant, but it is not morally charged. Viruses merely act out a type of inherent program devoid of any self-understanding or intent, and you happened to have had the rotten luck of taking one into your body.

Finally, what of the earthquakes, hurricanes, tornadoes, tsunamis, and other unexpected natural disasters ending thousands of human lives and destroying our property? Surely these are evil? Devastating, dreadful, wounding, yes, but they are not evil. Natural disasters are just things that happen on an old and geologically active planet, floating in a temporary universe tending to disorder. Only where the mind is intelligent enough to understand its own actions and the effects of those actions can right and wrong be formulated.

Bad things happen. Animals and insects wound people, plants cause rashes, bacteria and viruses cause pain and sap life, and natural disasters spread suffering and destruction but these acts are not immoral. The elements are indifferent and unconscious, so they cannot produce evil. Neither do the life forms that harm us have the understanding needed to produce a truly evil action, at least as far as we know.

Just as evil does not exist in the world neither does good. Flowers produce pleasant smells, the skies are tinted a soft blue, and the earth is filled with beauties and pleasures for the mind to enjoy, yet these are not good; not in a moral sense.

Even when we move from the material world to the human mind, we are not instantly taken to a place where all is good or evil. There are those who insist all things are either a virtue or a sin, but when one objectively considers the issue they find this is not the case.

The material items and technologies of the human world are neutral and only express the good or evil found in the minds controlling them. For example, planes are completely indifferent, and even making them into a war plane does not corrupt them, because wars can be just or unjust. Even when the plane is used to bomb an innocent city, it is not to be considered evil. It was the human mind that constructed it and human intent that guided it. As it is with planes so it is with all other things in life. Everything in the material world is neither good nor evil, but used by good or evil minds to accomplish their ends.

Morality is based in the mind of the viewer, and to show this I will use the example of a naked human body. Is the uncovered body of a man or a woman inherently good or evil? No, the body simply is, and if someone uses it for evil then it is the owner's mind that is the problem. Also, when someone thinks evil things as they look upon a naked body, then the problem is in the viewer's mind.

I know this might be hard to accept at first due to the taboos our culture has filled us with, but consider the example of a male gynecologist who looks at the bodies of naked women on a daily basis. Every day the doctor sees the ladies in compromising positions, positions that can even be sexually suggestive, but does this make him evil? People on the outside may say yes or no, but the deciding factor is not public opinion, it is the mental activities of the doctor. If in his mind he is in total control and dedicated to the bettering of his patient, then viewing the naked form is pure from beginning to end. However, if he is filled with lewd motives and thoughts regarding the ladies, though his actions may promote health, his mind is committing harm.

The goodness or evil of a thought or deed is rooted in the mind of the doer. It is easy for us to come along and condemn someone who we see as less virtuous than ourselves, or sternly correct one we are certain is doing wrong. Nevertheless, the person we are condemning could know something we do not, or lack a piece of knowledge we possess. In the first case, we need to stop our mouths and learn. In the second, we need to remember our own imperfections and kindly enlighten them.

There are some actions requiring little deliberation in order to determine if they are right or wrong. Examples of this can be found in the genocide conducted by the Nazi party, the hate crimes of the Ku Klux Klan, and the false justice of Dark Age Catholicism. However, there are some actions those on the outside cannot comment on, because they are matters of personal preference.

Maybe you think a song I am listening to has too fast a beat, the symbols on my shirt are evil, or I spent too much money on my car. However, it could be you did not take the time to hear the meaning of the song, and so did not realize its merit. Perhaps, you did not understand the symbols, and so did not realize their virtue. Or maybe you did not know my car was the last gift my grandpa ever gave me. We cannot judge the moral nature of every action taken by those around us, because we do not know all the factors involved.

We are all on completely different levels of understanding, and if we try to expand the understanding of another too quickly we can break them. Also, if we try to pull them down to our level we can cause them to crumble. It is for this reason we must understand that the goodness or evil of a thing is based upon one's level of understanding. When someone is lacking understanding, it is our place to instruct and cultivate their mind, not insult and condemn them.

It has taken me a long time to understand goodness and evil are really just correct and incorrect. It is wisdom versus ignorance, rather than holy versus unholy; a matter of truth and error instead of virtue and sin. The reason a thing is *good* or *evil* is because of the affects it has on the doer, and the world around them. If a thought or action does harm, arises from ignorance, and is out of harmony with the natural flow of the universe, then it should be avoided and eliminated from the mind. Likewise, if a thought or action helps, arises from understanding, and is in tune with the symphony of life, then it should be sought out and instilled in our characters.

We have to get beyond limited cultural views of right and wrong, and into the flow of reality. If an idea is pure or an action correct, it is because its nature is *purity* and *correctness*. A thing is not made right or wrong by the words of prophets, teachers, or gods, a thing is right because it *is* right and wrong because it *is* wrong. This means the ideas, entities, and actions of life are not to be judged right or wrong by some superimposed religious or philosophical principle, rather they are to be judged based on how they affect reality.

There are reasons why evil things are not good to do - they cause harm, disorder, and disrupt the flow of life creating difficulty. It is not that evil is a delightful thing we are being banned from, it is something that will destroy us and all we love. There are good reasons for making sure our thoughts and actions are correct. If we do not understand those reasons, if we are just complying to the standards of good and evil held forth by the culture we live in so we will be accepted by those around us or loved by some supernatural being, then we are spiritual parrots who chirp back to their preachers and gurus the things that will get us crackers. This type of spirituality is worthless because it is not personal, and whenever we are faced with the choice between correct and incorrect action, we will choose poorly because the only lesson we learned from our religion was how to conform to the ideas of those around us and be rewarded for it.

There is one reality, and it is not split into good and evil. There is one universal flow produced by the simultaneous motion of all things. As this reality moves, it creates moments and every moment presents those living in it with choices about how they are to conduct themselves. In each moment, there is a course of action that will create harmony, perpetuate wisdom, and benefit all involved - this path is the correct path - it is the way the wise walk. At the same time, in each moment there are courses of action that will create disunity, perpetuate ignorance, and harm all those involved - these are the incorrect paths - they are the ways walked by fools.

If I choose the correct path, I will keep myself in harmony with the flow of the universe and squarely in the way of truth. When I walk this path I am helped by those around me. They return the kindness I freely give, and I am free of guilt because I have done no harm in thought, word, or deed. The longer I walk this path the better I become, the more I benefit myself and others, and the deeper my joy. Reality is beautiful and free, because the way of truth makes me free and beautiful.

However, if I choose an incorrect path I will put myself out of harmony with the flow of the universe and squarely in the path of illusion. When I walk a wrong path, I hurt myself and others with incorrect actions and thoughts. This causes me to receive hurt from those around me, and I am filled with guilt and sorrow because my thoughts are incorrect, my words tear down, and my deeds do harm. The longer I walk this path the worse I become, the more pain I create in my life and the lives of others, and the deeper my despair grows.

Reality is ugly and unpleasant, because the way of illusion has made me unpleasant and ugly.

It is not that those who experience heaven are in a different reality than those who taste hell, it is just the first group have a nature in harmony with reality and the second does not. It is the difference between a sober man who knowingly jumps from the boat to frolic in the lake, and his drunken twin who falls in the lake after consuming too much alcohol. The first floats freely, feels joy, and has their life refreshed by the waves. The second splashes wildly, feels horror, and suffocates beneath the waters.

Were they not in the same lake? Did they both not enter the water with a splash? What then made the one live and the other die? It was their mentality and action. This is the same as it is with reality. Those who harmonize with the truth are embraced by Heaven and earth, while those who reject the truth are vomited out of the earth and crushed by Heaven.

Better Than Good

Young Man had tried repeatedly to best Old Beauty in feats of reasoning and knowledge, but time and again she showed her superiority. One day, Young Man thought he had finally crafted a riddle Old Beauty could not answer. Walking to her tent he looked her in the eye and ask, "What is better than good?" Old Beauty smiled, she never tired of Young Man's attempts to stump her, and it was nice to see her friend was thinking deeply.

After thinking for a moment she replied, "Good is too much a matter of opinion and perspective to be of much use, understanding and truth excel it in every way." Young Man looked skeptical, so Old Beauty began a parable to demonstrate her point, "One day, there was a good woman in a village who fell ill. This woman gave a lot of her time and wealth to make the lives of those in the village better. All were sad she was sick and called for a monk to pray for her. The monk fasted for three days, and pleaded for Heaven to make this beloved woman well. However, his prayers seemed to do no good. The monk was a good man, with a good mind, and good motives, but Heaven did not seem to answer, and the only thing he could do was keep praying."

"On the morning of the fourth day a very wise doctor passed by. He had been at a nearby village treating a sick man, and would have traveled on, but hearing the prayers of the monk he decided to see what would make a man call so strongly for Heaven's intervention. The doctor made his way to the crowd where the monk was praying, there he was told what was happening and his heart was touched. After examining the patient for a moment, he went over to his backpack, took out the herbs to treat the ailment, gave them to the woman, and waited to see if she improved."

"The next morning the woman was better, and all marveled at the power of herbs to heal. The woman thanked the monk and the doctor, as did the town people, and they turned to leave. However, as they were leaving the doctor heard someone mocking Heaven and the monk for appealing to it. The doctor stopped, looked them squarely in the eyes, and said, "You mock the monk? Do you not know that his prayers are what brought me here? Faith is the gate through which truth, knowledge, and wisdom enter. Once these have arrived, faith is no longer needed, but still I would not say Heaven is not involved. Did you make the herbs my friend? Did you give to mortals the tools of understanding? Wisdom and fact are far better than childlike goodness and faith, but they are no reason to mock Heaven."

Chapter Thirteen

When you hear the words *good* and *evil*, they usually are not being used correctly. Whenever one says *good* they usually mean what their native philosophical or religious system has told them is right, or what gives them pleasant feelings and enjoyable experiences. Likewise, whenever one says *evil*, they usually mean what the group of people and system of understanding they were born into tell them is bad, or what causes them pain.

To use *good* and *evil* in the ways shown above is like using the word *scrape* to describe getting your arm cut off, or saying you are *hungry* to describe the feeling in your belly when you have not eaten for ten days. Such shallow and culturally biased definitions must be thrown out the window if we are ever going to understand what *good* and *evil* really are.

In the next two chapters, we are going to remove from *good* and *evil* the incorrect cultural definitions we have had drilled into our minds from birth. Then, we are going to put them where they belong, back onto the life altering cosmic forces they are supposed to describe.

Good

In order to understand anything, we must first define it correctly, and in a way not limited by cultural ideas or narrow systems of thought. Therefore, our first duty as we begin to explore goodness is to define it correctly.

Good is the mental and moral force that creates and is created by truth. This meta-substance improves the mind, body, and circumstances of those who immerse themselves in it, while inspiring respect for the life and freedom of all living things. When I speak of *good* action, I mean an action benefiting all living things. When I speak of *good* thought, I mean thoughts that are accurate. I am not speaking of invisible beings or supernatural forces.

Whenever humans learn anything, it comes to us from a pool of available information. For example, when I was a child if I wanted to learn about frogs my pool of available information was the ideas of those around me, what I could learn from books they provided me with, and what I could learn myself by watching the frogs near my home. Goodness then is the pool of accurate information anyone anywhere could ever be exposed to. The pool is all the truth humanity has ever learned or can learn. This pool is contained in our mind, the minds of the people around us, and in those things humans record their thoughts on such as videos, books, audio recordings, carvings, pictures, and the like.

This true information can only be experienced or altered by minds able to perceive and understand it. Dogs, cats, birds, and all the other creatures on earth do not concern themselves with right and wrong. The power to fathom and express truth, or to understand and express error, as far as we know belongs only to one set of beings on earth - humans.

It has been the habit of people to divide *good* into a list of virtues containing, but not limited to, the states of mind and action represented by the words: wisdom, beauty, kindness, mercy, purity, gentleness, justice, forgiveness, patience, self-control, compassion, humility, and understanding. In reality *goodness* is not a multitude of things it is only truth manifesting itself according to the circumstance. When I am speaking truth it is expressed as humility, patience, wisdom, and gentleness. When I am in a friendship with you it is expressed as trust, honesty, understanding, and forgiveness. Then, when I am a student it is expressed as attentiveness, punctuality, openness, and respect.

Truth is one substance that appears differently according to its environment, just as water is ice in one environment but steam in another. When one comes into contact with, or internalizes any part of truth they touch all of it. This is comparable to listening to a good song. When I hear the beginning, and I like it, I continue listening to the song, and thus am pulled deeper into it until I have heard the whole thing. The difference is truth is an endless melody, as long as you listen and dance to its tune you will be continually drawn deeper into it.

Another way of understanding the oneness of truth is comparing it to a tree. The leaf is connected to the limb, connected to the trunk, connected to the root. All parts together form the tree. Likewise, compassion is the highest expression of wisdom, wisdom is the ultimate kindness, kindness is humble, humility is merciful, mercy is just, justice brims with understanding, understanding is power, and the greatest power of all is compassion. Together they are truth.

Truth, like the tree, is living and when it is cultivated in the mind and expressed in action it grows. Any segment of truth you come to understand is a door leading you deeper into its mysteries. Humility leads you to wisdom, wisdom reveals the practicality of compassion, compassion leads you to understand the need for justice, justice teaches you the reason for equality, equality leads you to new understanding, and by understanding one obtains self-control.

Truth is the path all humanity should walk, and reality is the visible expression of it. If we would all follow the path of truth, there would be total freedom for each member of the human race and peace would reign. Just as an ant colony flows in flawless harmony because selflessness it the root of every action, so would humanity flow in flawless harmony if each of us would make truth the root of every thought and action.

Truthfulness in mind and motion is the birthright of humanity, and the path we must take in order to be in harmony with ourselves, others, and the universal flow. It is a crime against our kind to make the motives and actions of less intelligent beings the model of human conduct.

Our age has taken the psychology of beasts and placed it at the root of all human behavior. Actions flowing from a mind filled with compassion for others are attributed to a subconscious drive to save our genes. Expressions of kindness are reduced to social networking for personal gain, and should one refuse to accept such explanations it is seen as a failure to accept our true nature. If I treat a bird like a fish, and put it in a tank of water it will die, because by nature it cannot breathe water.

Likewise, if I treat a dog like a bird, and throw it over the mountainside so it can fly free it will die, because by nature it cannot soar. The needs of each creature are determined by its nature. To try to understand the nature of humanity by comparing and contrasting us to any other creature on earth, will lead us to the same unfortunate results at putting birds under water or tossing dogs from cliffs. What works well for other living creatures, does not work well in the realm of humanity.

Making another hungry so I can be full, cold so I can be warmed, or miserable so I can have comfort is considered to be the natural way of things. "Survival of the fittest" it is said, and then wise, aware, and intelligent human beings set about acting like animals and excusing themselves for it. What greater injustice could be conducted against our race than the denial of our unique natures and superior minds?

Humanity's place and needs are determined by human nature, and cannot be deduced by watching other creatures, just as one cannot know the needs of a frog by studying a mouse or the nature of a tree by studying cows. *Survival of the fittest* does not make for human betterment, it makes for human destruction. We cannot survive by seeking what is best for ourselves at the expense of another. We survive by making the good of others equal to our own. The only reason why this doesn't work as it should is because the majority of humans act like beasts. They do not understand themselves.

Can you imagine how the world would be if each and every person made the needs of other people equal to their own? There would be no want or poverty, all of us would have everything we need and more. Greed, selfishness, and all other manifestations of ignorance are cosmic disorders that generate suffering, decay, and death on a world wide scale. Truth is the cure for this disease, as well as the best way to live. Those who refuse to seek out and infuse their life with the virtues of truth, live lives that are merely painful walks to death.

The idea truth does not exist is at the root of all human suffering. Moral relativity - accurately stating my idea of truth is not your idea of truth - has been twisted into meaning truth is whatever I want it to be. As people try to apply this principle, they end up believing and acting out lies. Thus, people create misery for themselves and all around them. While it is accurate to say what I have been taught from birth will influence what I think is true, it is not accurate to say truth is a matter of opinion.

Due to the different cultural influences each of us is exposed to, we all have different ideas about what truth is, but these are just inner realities. In the external reality, each and every human being on the face of the earth shares the same mental needs, just as they share the same physical needs. The need for beauty, freedom, a clear conscience, kindness, and forgiveness is built into the human mind as deeply as our need for food and drink. There are different cultural ways of fulfilling these needs - different religions, philosophies, and customs - just as there are different ways of cooking food, but the need in both cases is the same.

Truth is not a cultural perspective, it is accurate information that should govern the flow of the human mind and be the root of every action. Remember what we learned about ideas? Every idea has its own internal nature, causing each idea to affect human consciousness in a unique way, and as we express our ideas they change reality.

Truth in all its forms provides the elements needed for a healthy mind, just as food in all its forms provides the elements needed for a healthy body. When one does not use the mental elements of reality in the correct way, the mind will sicken and suffer, just as the body does without food.

When the human mind experiences compassion, wisdom, self-control, kindness, and mercy it makes these mental substances a part of itself. Truth is made a part of consciousness, and through consciousness a part of life. Mind becomes deep and pure, life becomes beautiful and clear, and the total being is made healthy.

The pool of truth - the ocean of information that teaches a correct view of reality and brings the self into harmony with the flow of eternity - is the privilege of every human being to drink from. Those who take the time to seek and apply the truth to their lives become peaceful people experiencing a beautiful reality.

This tranquil splendor is experienced by all who align themselves with the forces and flow of the universe. Just as all rivers come from and return to the oceans, so do the ideas and actions giving life come from the waters of right understanding.

Unfortunately however, wherever there is a correct way of doing things there is unavoidably an incorrect way of doing things. Wherever there is a being with high enough mental capacity to produce truth, in the same being there is the opportunity to produce error. This certainly is the case with humanity. Our world contains goodness and truth, but it also contains evil and illusion.

Worse Than Evil

A week had passed since Young Man had riddled Old Beauty, and it seemed time to try again. He knew it would probably result in learning something, but he loved learning and found Old Beauty's stories very interesting, so he did not mind. Thinking of another question he thought would give her trouble, Young Man journeyed till he found her outside the tent, beating her rugs with a broom made of small limbs and leaves.

After greeting her, and inquiring how her day had been going he asked, "What is worse than evil?" By this time Old Beauty figured he was just trying to get a story out of her. However, she didn't mind, because she liked telling the stories as much as he liked hearing them. After thinking for moment she replied, "Wisdom and truth misused are far worse than evil."

Young Man was inclined to believe her, but wanting proof and another tale asked, "Can you demonstrate for me why?" Old Beauty smirked and began, "Once there was a very greedy man who wanted to be chief of his village, but the spot was already occupied by his uncle. Wanting rid of his uncle he decided to hire a master of evil magic to slay his uncle in a secret way. The greedy man knew where to find just such a person, and after enlisting the services of the evil worker, brought the witch doctor into his home to do the rite."

"The witch doctor laid out his tools, and set about right away to weave a curse nothing could prevent from accomplishing its goal. The man lived far away from the village, and so did not think the loud chanting would be noticed by anyone. However, an assassin who was tired of his trade had just moved in above him. The assassin patiently waited for the noise to stop, but it did not. Infuriated by the seemingly ceaseless din, he gathered his tools, and set out to find the source of the racket disturbing his peace."

"When the assassin arrived at the greedy man's hut, he saw the devil bringer, recognized the bloody symbols, and instantly knew what was happening. Summoning the home owner the assassin said to him, "It is clear your intent is evil, and it is clear you have found another as devoted to doing wickedly as yourself, but why do you try to deal death by such unenlightened means? Here, I have a poison that will kill a man one week after he takes it. I am tired of killing, I am tired of harm, and I wish for peace so I might make peace with myself. If you will stop this infernal din I will give you the poison at a good price, and you may accomplish your evil. The greedy man was delighted at such a clean solution. He paid the assassin his price, collected the means to accomplish his evil, and thought to himself, 'Indeed the dark magic worked well'."

Chapter Fourteen

Evil is not a word describing a skiing accident, a plane crash, or a sudden fall resulting in death. Though all these things are bad, they do not meet the criteria for evil. My mom may make me eat vegetables as a child, but as long as she is patient, loving, and fair about it, this is not an evil thing, though I greatly dislike it. *Evil* is the mental and moral force that creates and is created by error.

Error makes the situations, bodies, and minds it fills suffer and die. Even though error can grant temporary pleasure and benefit, it does so at the expense of the life expressing it. When I say an action is evil or erroneous, I mean it is out of harmony with the universal flow of reality, and brought about by a misunderstanding of reality itself.

Just as in the case of *good,* we are not discussing some unseen supernatural agent, we are talking about a single pool of data formed from the ideas and actions of humanity, kept alive in our records and memories, and spread by our interactions with others.

Just as humanity divided truth into a list of qualities to be sought after, so have they divided error into a list of acts and ways of thinking that ought to be avoided. Lies, foolishness, cruelty, harshness, corruption, hate, pride, and ignorance are some of the forms of error. This division, however much it may help us to understand the manifestations of error, leads us away from the fact that error is a single undivided force just as truth is.

One thing manifesting itself in many ways may be hard to grasp, but again water leads us to a better understanding. When water freezes it becomes ice, when it boils it becomes steam, and when it is between extremes it is a river, a beverage, or an ocean. In one circumstance it is a solid, in another it is a gas, and in another a liquid, but it is always water. In all instances it is still hydrogen mixed with oxygen, just as all virtue is an expression of truth in action, and all vice is only error in motion.

When all is cool, error manifests as pride, arrogance, or disrespect. When things are starting to heat up, error emerges in the forms of hate, rage, and murder. Finally, when things are meandering along their usual course, error appears as indifference, lack of self-control, and waste. No matter what form it takes, evil is always erroneous ideas prompting the mind to bring them into reality through act.

Error is one as truth is one. When we allow any part of it into our life we have accepted all of it. Whenever I am full of pride I also hold the seeds of anger, because if my pride is hurt my rage will rise to defend me. As I nourish pride, I also nourish the seeds of fear. I fear I will lose the abilities I am proud of, or the things they earn me.

Error is a perversion of the natural order. If truth is an inspirational and stirring symphony, then error is an intoxicating lullaby. Eventually, as one observes and studies the mechanics of error, they will come to see hate and apathy as high forms of ignorance. Ignorance breeds foolishness and fear, fear gives rise to anger and injustice, injustice gives rise to hate and apathy, and apathy leads to decay and death.

Error is one united force that feeds upon itself, and pulls those who participate in it deeply into its toxic delights. Those who are made to lie soon after become fearful, fear breeds worries, worry compounds guilt, and guilt is covered by abuses and more lies.

Evil, once understood, is the highest form of ignorance and a way of living all humanity ought to avoid, like a dirty needle or a poisoned goblet. The needle and the goblet may contain things with the power to grant a sweet experience, but in the end they will destroy and take away from us not only the best things in life but life itself.

Error places those who commit it out of harmony with the cosmic flow. They are made a dead note in the song of life, the broken bone in the body called humanity. Error grows from the root of selfishness, and when one sets out to obtain their desires regardless of how it will affect themselves or others, disunity and harm to all can be the only result. If I behave unjustly, my injustice calls to the worst parts of the person I have wronged. If they are not an enlightened being they will have an erroneous response. This establishes cycles of suffering only correct action and right thinking can break. As long as selfishness is the mode of operation, only unhappiness and suffering will come to pass.

Not only does error create disunity, it also breeds slavery. It makes slaves of others through fear, force, and manipulation, just as it makes self its slave through addiction, greed, and pride. Any who dwell in fear, ignorance, hate, intemperance, or self-love will not see prosperity or peace as long as they continue in wrong thoughts and deeds.

Error is disharmony with the natural flow, and a path no human should take. Yet, it still seems to be the most popular road. This road has been made even more popular in the recent past, due to a misunderstanding of truth and cultural relativity. It is accurate to say what one culture calls *right* another calls *wrong,* but this doesn't mean truth and error do not exist. Truth will better, uplift, and heal any human mind if it is taught in a kind and understandable way, while error will destroy, depress, and wound any human who clings to it.

Right and wrong are not relics of ancient fools, or the imagining of undeveloped savages, they are facts about reality the thinkers of old saw and understood, and they are still active in our world today. It is not these facts are hard to see, it is in our pride and misunderstanding we have neglected the simplest and deepest lessons of truth, until they have been almost forgotten.

If ever we are to be happy and whole, we must understand the realness of error personally by study, observation, and reflection. Error is the ultimate virus, it moves from mind to mind, corrupting the purity of memory and conscience as it wounds the flesh.

The need for beauty, peace, freedom, joy, and every other color in the spectrum of truth is wired into our very nature. Error and its many manifestations - called vices - destroy and wreck our minds and lives. How can one be at peace when they are full of fear and lies? How can one have self-respect and confidence when they know themselves to be perverted, hateful, and uncaring? How can one possess freedom when the esteem and opinions of others keeps them from doing what they know to be right? How can one have joy, while they recall how they unjustly took joy from another?

Wrong information is a poison and a disease. When it enters the mind the whole systems of thought is made ill, even though at times the illness is sweet. When I am in trouble a lie can help me escape the consequences of my actions, when I am depressed abuse of drugs can temporarily mask the pain, and when I am starving inside sexual pleasure can give me temporary fullness. Yet, these perks are short lived. The lie is found out and the consequences are more severe, the drugs wear off and the pain and circumstances I was trying to escape have become worse, and the glow given by sexual encounter wears off leaving me emptier than I was before.

Whenever we invite hate, foolishness, intemperance, cruelty, injustice, and pride into our minds, these mental elements change our mental makeup. As mind grows accustomed to wrong thinking, we begin to see our ideas as okay, so we no longer hesitate to make them a reality through action. In this way, our life becomes filled with the fruit of seeds we have planted, and eventually we sit in a garden of joyless misery.

The tides of error rolling across our world - these twisted ways of seeing ourselves, reality, and others - can be seen, tested, understood, and avoided. If we allow wrong inside of us we will do wrongly, and put ourselves out of harmony with all parts of reality. How can we prevent this from happening? By immersing our minds in the quest for truth, and making the truths we find the basis of all our actions. Those who run to truth run from error, and those who run to evil run from good.

It is not just for out benefit we should strive to leave all corruption behind. Those who are filled with vice and wrong will taint all they hold dear. Seeing the misery they have caused, they will themselves become more miserable. On the other hand, those who avoid error and acquire truth will not only find and experience the best in life they will share it with others. As they see the good they have done to others blossom into joy and prosperity, they themselves will become wealthier and more joyous.

Measuring Right and Wrong

One day, Young Man heard a knock on his door and opening it saw was Old beauty. He was very surprised but honored she would take the time to come see him. Young Man asked, "To what do I owe this honor?" Old Beauty replied, "I was concerned you might have misunderstood something I said". "What would that be?", inquired Young Man, to which Old Beauty replied, "Even though good and evil have been tainted by social custom and cultural bias, I do not want to you to think right and wrong do not exist."

Young Man was inspired by his teacher's devotion to true sayings, and after making her comfortable, invited her to speak her mind. Old Beauty gladly accepted, and began her tale, "Once there were two fish in a school who went to explore a cove. Their names were Skidder and Finny. Both of them were very bright fish, and each enjoyed racing around the ocean floor and finding new things. After making their way to the cove, they played for some time among the rocks and fallen coconuts floating there on the ocean's surface."

"The two fish played and played, until the sun made its way down to the horizon. Even though they were in a college-level school, they did not want to worry those who cared for them, and so determined to head back home. However, even though the sun was sinking they still had not gotten all of the play out of their system, so they decided to make the trip home a race. They counted to three, and then shot towards their colony on the ocean floor."

"All their lives each of the fish had been told not to swim near the surface of the water in the evening. It was said a group of trident bearing angels in the area had learned the art of fishing, and loved the taste of fish. However, this superstitious warning did not matter to Finny because he was a very fast fish, very smart, and very proud. He wanted to beat Skidder no matter what, even if it meant cheating and taking a little risk. Finny knew about a short cut through the rock formation separating the bay from their home. The fish of his colony used it to beat other fish to the water-beetles that played at the bay in the noon-day sun. If he would go that way, he would beat Skidder with no problem."

"Finny began to swim as fast as he could. He worried a bit the angels might get him, but he banished such childish proverbs from his thoughts. Instead, he imagined all the glory he would have at school when they all heard he had beaten Skidder - the fastest fish on the coast. By the time Finny saw the entrance to the shortcut, he was moving so fast he was almost flying. His mind began to fill with thoughts of all the girls that would adore him for beating the champ, and how jealous all the boys would be at spawning time. Just as his mental fantasies reached their peak, just as he was about to enter the passage, a sudden and magnificent pain ripped through him. Finny watched the ocean shrink beneath him, and in the *final moments of his life knew himself to be in the clutches of an owl, what the old fish called a, "trident carrying angel".*

"There are things called good that are meaningless ancient social customs, and then there are ancient instructions that prevent suffering and cause life to prosper. The wise devote themselves to separating what is sound counsel from what is useless dogma, and those who do not take the time to do so become owl food."

Chapter Fifteen

To the eye that has not looked deeply, it appears as though there have been thousands of wars down through time, but in reality there has been only one - the conflict between truth and error. As far back into human history as we can go, the struggle between right and wrong has raged in the minds and motives of mortals. Even in our age of extreme understanding and sophisticated technology, this fundamental conflict shows no sign of ending.

Every moment we live, we must decide if we are going to do right or wrong. From the time we wake up, we are bombarded with millions of choices regarding what we are going to that day. Will we be bringers of help or bearers of suffering? Every instant this question is asked us and how we answer it determines who we are, what we will become, and what impact we will have on our world now and in the future.

Some see the question of morality in terms of utility. If you live ethically, then you will keep your job, feed your family, and avoid the punishment of the government. Some see the question of morality in terms of duty. If you do not act rightly, then others will think bad of you, you will bring shame on your family, or you will fail the task fate has given you. Still others see morality in terms of spiritual principles. If I do not act rightly, God will be angry with me, I will miss heaven, or I will arrive at hell. Finally, there are those who see the question of morality as a list of useless behaviors people do because of cultural programming - going so far as to say right and wrong do not exist. Are any of these the *right* way of looking at right and wrong, or does it even matter?

In reality, the question of right and wrong impacts the areas of utility, duty, spirituality, and personal preference, but transcends them all. To see morality in only one of these veins is to be blind to the others. What we need, and what this chapter seeks to give, is a unifying vision of the *whys* and *why nots* of truth and error. Without such a vision we will find ourselves doing things merely because someone we trust said so. If you do not see the harm in this, I would point you to the dark ages of Europe and the dark years of Nazi Germany. At that time, grave wrongs were done by the common folk because their leaders assured them what they were doing was holy and right.

Good and evil are not understood as they should be. We all have ideas about what to do and what not to do. For those who do not want to think about it much, there are hundreds of spiritual, philosophical, and political systems ready to provide all the answers. However, as I look into these systems from the outside, I wonder how many people within them could demonstrate the truth of their ideas?

It has been my experience very few can give a good, solid, and logical reason why what they call evil is error, and what they call good is truth. The rest of this chapter is a demonstration of the principles I have set forth, so you may know their truthfulness. We will compare nine forms of error to nine forms of truth and see which are the most beneficial.

Wrath and Peace

Wrath is not anger. Anger is a natural emotion that passes through us when we feel as though we have been wounded, insulted, or treated in a manner we consider unjust. There are times when anger is justified, but it must always be rooted in truth, filled with awareness, and guided by wisdom.

Wrath is what happens when anger has forsaken truth, blinded reason, and robbed us of understanding. When one has not disciplined the mind and filled it with truth, wrath will often take the place of anger. No matter where you are or what type of human you are, if your mind becomes filled with wrath, nothing but ill will come of it.

Wrath overreacts and gives no thought to the consequences of its actions, so its effects are harmful and at times deadly. It is closely related to pride, fear, and impatience. It flows easily from the mind where these disharmonies have been allowed to take root.

One of the biggest reasons wrath is bad, is due to the principle of replication - how like brings forth like. If you are taken by rage and let it pour into the moment, this same attitude is going to be awakened in the minds of others and returned to you. If you cut me with a knife I may draw a gun, if you harm me I may kill you, and if you kill me my family could kill you and your family.

Even if goodness has become the root of action in the mind of the one you attack, and in the hearts of those who hold them dear, there are still going to be unpleasant consequences. One of these could be the wrath of the legal system. The justice of governments will take your money, your freedom, or your life depending on the amount of harm you have caused.

If you explode in a rage at work you could lose your job, if you explode on your wife and children you could lose your family, and if you explode in an empty room you could lose yourself. In all times and places, wrath is an incorrect action, and no matter who or where you are bad consequences are sure to come. Wrath wounds those who allow it to inform their actions; it is total disharmony with the way of things.

When the mind is filled with guilt, greed, pride, shame, and selfishness, it is quick to flare up and defend itself, quick to protect its gain, and quick to lash out when experiencing inner turmoil. However, when the mind has sought, acquired, and applied the full spectrum of truth, love for the material realm fades, because it is seen for what it is. Pride turns to humility when self understands its limits, and there is no shame because the individual lives in a manner not to be ashamed of. Also, self is no longer our primary interest, the well-being of others is made just as important as our own, and so we act in ways providing the greatest benefit for all. Truth in mind and action gives peace, because purity within helps us to be in harmony with ourselves and others, while wisdom frees us from the unrest of craving.

When filled with wrath the mind is like a turbulent ocean, thrashing all who enter it, and dashing its self restlessly against the rocks. However, when filled with peace the mind is like a calm ocean, carrying all who enter it places they could not have reached otherwise, while keeping itself whole.

Peace is superior to wrath in every way and is closely related to purity, wisdom, humility, and fearlessness. When the mind is filled with peace, it can deal with all situations quickly and clearly. From peace the mind reaches out with wisdom and not with blind passion.

In wrath, the principle of replication multiplies woes, but in peace it multiplies benefits. The peace our mind contains pours into the environment around us. When someone starts to curse and swear at us, rather than doing the same, the peace in us lets us speak softly. This softness dilutes the situation, and reduces the possibility of great harm. Even if the other party is still full of wrath, our peace empowers us to walk away. In this way, we avoid the cycle of escalation.

Peace makes what would otherwise be unbearable a joy, and prevents us from ruining ourselves or our relationships with unkind actions and words. Peace helps us to live long lives, it lets us absorb the stress and hardship of any circumstance and convert it to wisdom and experience. Peace is a universally helpful and needed part of the human condition.

Patience and Impatience

Patience is peace in action. It is how truth is expressed when I am enduring the mistakes of self and others, when I am waiting for a desired outcome, or when I am working to achieve a goal. When one is patient they do not act upon the first idea that bursts into their mind. They wait and allow the impulse to fade, so wisdom can determine the course of action instead of impulse.

Patience, and the need of it, is a lesson all about us in the natural world. If one is to make diamonds, they must wait patiently so the pressure and heat of the earth can reshape the coal. If one hopes to reap a beautiful harvest, they must work patiently and move with the seasons. They cannot become rushed, or force the plants to grow. If one is to make a beautiful mind and life for their self or others, they must work and wait patiently. The warping of human nature and the material world has been going on a long time. We must not expect changes to come overnight, or lose our calm while working to achieve them.

The patient being is one who has learned murmuring only darkens their own mind and the minds near them, so they do not complain. The patient mind also realizes haste only complicates things. There are times to act with speed, but acting speedily with calmness, information, and clarity is not the same as reactively blundering about in a situation. Not only this, but the patient mind does not lose focus or allow itself to become restless. It sits reflectively, and allows things to run their course.

What benefit is it to be free of complaint, restlessness, and sudden reaction? It allows us to listen without rush, to fix without harm, to see without blurring, and to speak without passion. Patience in all situations and at all times is the ideal, and it is totally achievable as long as we practice daily, and do not allow or inevitable failures to discourage us. Patience is the friend and teacher of every human. It is needed in the simplest mind as much as it is needed in the smartest.

What then is impatience? It is the state of not having patience, and though it doesn't always produce incorrect action it complicates everything. Even when impatience fails to create evil, those who allow it to remain in their mind will never realize their potential. They will be quick to complain, and so darken all situations they find their self in.

Just as the impatient are quick to complain, they are also slow of hearing. When another is trying to tell them something, they will not let the conversation run its course before commenting. Speaking impulsively they wound, and acting impulsively they harm and complicate.

Not only will the one who relishes impatience endure these things, they will hardly make a success of life. When things get tough they will bail out. This applies to all pursuits be they personal, professional, or spiritual. Likewise, when things take longer than desired they will just quit, accepting the slow rate of progress as failure. In this way, they miss out on the best joys, insights, and accomplishments life has to offer. The gardener refusing to cultivate the rose will never bring forth or enter into all her beauty.

To those who are patient all things are as they should be, and what is not can be endured in way that creates a good outcome. However, to those who are impatient nothing is ever as it should be, and good outcomes are the creation of chance or the wisdom of another. It does not matter if one lives life in a mansion or a rice patty, without patience they may as well be half dead.

Craving and Contentment

Life at times does not seem fair. However, since we cannot do anything about it, the only option left open to us is to learn how to be content regardless of what we have. Those who learn how to be content in all circumstances do not have their minds clogged by wishes for something else, or complaints about the present. They can dedicate their mental power to understanding how to live in this reality, and by understanding reality happiness can be attained.

The mind full of craving is destined to be filled with suffering, hardship, and unrest. When one is consumed with getting and maintaining, they never reflect on what they are or what they already have. They never gain understanding, and because of this, ignorant thoughts and actions keep them in misery.

Craving becomes wrong when the mind fixes itself on them. When one becomes passionate about acquiring and experiencing, they lose objectivity and forget wisdom. They do not consider as they should how their desires and actions affect themselves or others.

Unchecked lust also causes the object or event we are craving to appear more wonderful than it really is. We forget the good we have, and let our minds become filled with imaginings of what it would be like to satisfy our wants. As our imagination makes the object of our desire brighter and brighter, what we have already grows darker and darker, until we lose our spirit of gratitude. Once we no longer appreciate what we have, we begin to think if only we could get or experience the object of our affections, then we would be happy. This idea is completely wrong. Things can give us pleasure, but joy can only come from obtaining and practicing right understanding.

When one allows themselves to become attached to anything, they have opened a jar from which misery will always flow. The more the mind becomes flavored by its preferences, the more flavorless what it has becomes. Whatever bad experiences one may have to endure are made worse when our mind is allowed to pine away among useless hopes. The mind lost among wishes of escaping the pit never does, because it does not study how to do so.

As long as we do not curb our multitude of cravings and learn contentment, we will always fill our life with more and more things. The more things we have, the more loss we must experience in order to get them and keep them working. When the object of my desire breaks or runs out, my mind despairs and passionately seeks to replace it. The more objects I have sought and obtained the more this cycle will occur.

Now let us pause for a moment to consider what happens when the thing we deeply desire is gone, and we have no way to replace it? At the very best we will be dissatisfied. At the worst we will resort to harming others by taking what is not ours, or manipulating them to fulfill our cravings.

When we use others in this way we also hurt ourselves by committing acts causing us to lose our honesty, self-respect, freedom, and possibly our lives.

The more things we get, the more we complicate our mind and circumstance. This complexity causes us to divide our clarity, focus, and effort. As a result of these divisions, little is accomplished.

160

This is like the person who divides fourteen gallons of gas between seven vehicles. In the end the person is out of gas, and none of their vehicles will take them very far. The mind divided in this way further complicates what is already complex. It has less mental resources available to accomplish its goals or resolve problems. In this way, uncontrolled craving causes the rich to break themselves, and the poor to never be whole.

In our capitalistic world, there are millions of people trying to fill us with desires, so we might purchase their goods and services. Billions are spent every year on marketing and advertisement, so it is no wonder many brim with craving. It is far easier to allow desire to guide us than restraint, because by the time we are adults we have created habits of want and fulfillment. Since those around us behave in the same way, we believe this to be natural. Nevertheless, what is easiest is seldom best. It is like being on a raft floating down stream. It is easier to just let the current take you. However, when you get to the falls at the end of the river the hardships of paddling upstream no longer seem undesirable.

Those who think happiness, joy, and peace come from material objects and sensual desires are bound by lies. With these lies firmly implanted in their minds they go about spending time, freedom, health, and dignity to achieve their desires. Then they wonder why they are rushed, sick, enslaved, and full of self-hate. The reason of course is they have given away their riches to obtain rocks, devices, and sensual delights.

Where craving fails contentment succeeds. Contentment understands what wealth really is. The very things desire spent to obtain its wants - time, health, strength, intellect, and purity - are in reality the only true riches. Those who are enslaved by lust are victims of a bitter irony. They give away the things that make them happy in order to create happiness. This is like a bee keeper who trades all the bees they have for a jar of honey. For a time, the honey lasts, but then it is gone. They have nothing else to trade for more honey, and no longer possess those things needed to make it themselves.

Most of us are full of shame and regret, because we have hurt others and ourselves by acting ignorantly. Then, amid the sufferings we have created, we blame some supernatural entity, government, friend, thing, or circumstance for the situation our actions and choices have made. After this, we spend all we have in an effort to obtain a new religion, government, friend, thing, or circumstance only to end up more miserable than we were when we began. This is like the driver who buys another car, because the first one did not take them where they wanted to go. The diver is the problem and not the vehicle.

Those who fill their lives with truth realize they are responsible for all their problems. This empowers them to set about doing what is needed to fix their brokenness. Once the mind is fixed, the world is fixed as well. The problem was never external it was within us all along. The enlightened mind is a contented mind. It accepts everything in life as it is right now without corrupting it with wishes, hopes, wants, regrets, or fears. Contentment hinges upon realizing everything you need you already have or have access to. All improvement must come from within us, and change our inner selves if it is to last.

Contentment allows the mind to retain wisdom, so problems are solved with greater ease. It allows objectively to be retained, so one does not think with their emotions or in a narrow sighted way. As we think clearly, wisely, and peacefully we begin to act that way. As we mature in understanding, we refuse to harm another being, or forsake any part of truth in order to gain a temporary benefit. Because we have taken the time to become kind and calm, these same qualities are awakened in others and returned to us. As this attitude passes through society, all begin to work for the benefit of others. When we care for the dreams of others as much as we do our own, everyone achieves their dreams.

However, if one group becomes greedy, selfish, and attached they limit the flow of unity and goodness. This is why those devoted to goodness cannot prosper as they should. When one mind is filled with truth and awakens to goodness, twenty others filled with evil limit the influence of that mind. Yet, even though error and craving hinder truth, they cannot stop it. These are external forces, and as long as we choose to maintain truth within our mind, nothing outside us can take it away.

The contented mind can enjoy the material world in a way those bound to it never can. Realizing they do not need things to be happy, they can fully interact with anything, enhance their life with it, and then let it go. Thus, they can experience the pleasure of things without any of the suffering caused by lust.

The contented are able to avoid unnecessary complexity. They do not confuse want with need, so their life is simple. They are focused and put their time and money into things that matter, so they have a sense of accomplishment and self-respect. They are like the person who has one car filled with gas and enough wealth to fill it again and again. They can travel as far as they need to.

The contented know all things are created and destroyed moment by moment, so they do not become attached to them. They do not set about collecting piles of items that will only break and rust, neither do they lament when things rust and break.

It is exceedingly hard to be content when we are in a death camp starving, when our house has been destroyed by the forces of nature, and when death has taken someone we dearly love. However, as difficult as these things are, contentment must be maintained. Longing and attachment will not improve anything they will only make it worse.

No matter where the body is at, how it suffers, or what is lost, if the mind is pure and wise, the suffering is made bearable. Not only this, but by maintaining our composure in suffering, truth and peace can flow into all present. In this way, the environment is enlightened, the loss is less sharp, and we can ease the suffering of those around us.

Contentment is not cold and indifferent, it merely allows all things to come and go without preferring to have them or keep them away. The loss of freedom, possessions, loved ones, and the inability to meet our basic needs, are all tragedies to be lamented. Sorrow in these times is natural and even necessary, so we can come to terms with our grief. Contentment does not cause us to forsake natural emotions. Rather than strangling and killing our natural affections, contentment allows us to fully interact with them and then completely let them go.

Death, injustice, and disaster are elements of reality, but they are not the only elements. Life, fairness, and joy are also elements of reality, but these too are not the only ones. Most never get deeper than joy or sorrow, and as a result their existence is as good or as bad as they are happy or sad. Contentment allows us to get beyond these sets of extremes, and experience the full range of life while retaining a deep calm and satisfaction with living.

I may hurt horribly because I have lost my loved one, but deeper down I am at peace and filled with gratitude because I had the opportunity to love them at all. I may be pained as I walk among the rubble that used to be my home, yet I realize the moment is only a sentence on the page of my mind. The rest of the story has yet to be written. My body may unjustly ache and rot in the depths of a dungeon, but as I accept it without resentment, fear, or shame, I can retain mental freedom and inner peace.

Grudging and Forgiveness

To hold a grudge is like leaving a broken bone unfixed. The injury is always remembered, because the wound never stops aching. When we perceive a wrong has been done to us or by us, and we keep the unpleasant event forever in our mind - this is grudging. It is the friend of pride, shame, injustice, vengeance, and misunderstanding.

Whenever we hold a grudge, it is like the person who has a very strong piece of salt in their mouth that will never dissolve. Its savor overpowers any sweetness, and what is rotten becomes pleasant to the taste.

When I have done wrong, or have been done wrong, and refuse to let it go, I am letting the wrong forever hurt me and alter my actions. When a person has wounded me as a child and I refuse to forgive and let go, I am allowing that person to wound me afresh every day. When I have made a mistake and refuse to forgive myself, every morning I will be filled with new sorrow from wrongs I committed yesterday. This causes me to make even more mistakes, and darkens the color of all my experiences.

Who among us is flawless? Who among us has never erred? Who among us is forever beyond error? The wisest fail, the strongest weaken, and even the sun at times is eclipsed. Yet, the shadow passes, and the light always returns. If we will learn from our mistakes and let their shadows pass away, they will make us better than we were before. When we begrudge ourselves and others we make the path of life harder than it has to be, like a hiker who is carrying a bag of rocks. However, forgiveness is the scissor to free us of our burden.

Forgiveness is the friend of humility, understanding, and mercy. When we learn to forgive ourselves our minds become light and quick. We do not have to worry as we strive for excellence in morality, occupation, or understanding. We run without fear of falling and so we fall less. Those who do not forgive themselves pile error on error and shame upon shame until they are hateful, bitter, and depressed.

When we learn to forgive others, we free ourselves from them. The mistakes and errors of others no longer poison our minds and ruin our day. The wounds that have been made are able to heal, and the mind can again run through life without a limp.

It is important to note forgiving is not forgetting. Merely because I forgive a foolish friend for stealing my stuff, does not mean I forget what they have done. They have broken the silken string of trust, and though I love them and will help them as far as I can, it will take time and a definite change in them before the string is mended. Yet, even then it will never be exactly the same.

All wrong deeds and negative experiences should not be forgotten, because then we will learn nothing and all our suffering will have been in vain. We should not let bad things rob us of wholeness for the rest of our lives, nor should we let the faults of one individual destroy our interactions with others.

Cruelty and Kindness

The human mind has great potential to be violent towards its self and other living things. Cruelty means intentionally and unjustly causing harm to another living creature. It is the companion of prejudice, wrath, pride, and ignorance.

Harming with words, hurting with physical attacks, or imprisoning others in a cage made of bars or ideas leaves scars. Even the wounds themselves at times do not heal, because the harm does not stop, the wounded party dies, or the one who was hurt lacks the understanding and strength needed to mend the wounds. Once done, an act can never be taken back. The shadows it casts upon our life and others are long and deep.

When a person hurts what is harmless, attacks what is defenseless, and breaks what is much weaker than their self, they are destroying their own lives as well. The mind is filled with guilt due to their wrong actions. There are only two ways to deal with this guilt - either I give into it, seek forgiveness, and stop doing harm or I suffocate my conscience. If I choose the latter and refuse to correct my actions, more and more I make myself the slave of rage until I am helpless. Harsh and unkind actions become the habit of my life, and misery fills me and those I interact with.

Kindness has the opposite effect of cruelty. To be kind means to be gentle in all your actions and to make choices that heal and better all living things. Kindness is the brother of mercy and the companion of wisdom, reason, compassion, and strength.

Cruel words and actions harm and darken the lives of others, but kind actions heal and enlighten them. Kindness reaches out with softness to sooth aching minds, and helps them carry life's heavy burdens.

Hateful actions call forth hate, and kindness calls forth kindness. When you are sweet to others, if there is anything sweet in them they will return it to you. However, if they are only sour, then perhaps you can instill in them a bit of sweetness. Helping others causes them to help you, though this should not be your motive, and when you give hope to another you encourage yourself also. By being respectful and friendly, you carry a pleasant energy making life easier for all living things.

Rather than being filled with shame and devoid of self-respect, the person who is nice without ulterior motives is filled with peace, confidence, and a sense of dignity. A person who is helpful, free, and pure is able to deal with all the problems life throws at them. Also, when the problems become more than one person can bear, they will be more likely to have the assistance of others.

Kindness generates trust, mutual respect, and harmony. It has the power to remove the harm done by hateful actions, as water restores life to a parched plant. It is the privilege of every human to be kind, and make kindness the goal of every action.

Because so few accept this privilege, there is much pain and suffering. It is not the fault of any unseen supernatural agency that the world is unforgiving and harsh it is the fault of the humans in it. Occupied with our own profit, and controlled by our passions, we forbid others the help and mercy we would want if we were in the same circumstances as them. We think this will cause us to profit like the beasts that grow strong by feeding on the weak, but this is not the case.

We are not dogs who possess only limited awareness and instinct to guide us, and we are not vultures who by nature get fat on the death of other things. We are creatures with the capacity to understand, relate, help, and heal. When we fail to do these things, we are adding water to the flood of human suffering which already covers the earth. If we would help others regardless of their color, class, or creed, then our world would become something like the heaven we all long for.

Prejudice and Reason

Few things are more harmful than someone who thinks they know when they in fact have no idea. In one way, the mind works like a glass of water - if it is full of belief it can never be filled with fact. This is the exact state of those who are prejudice.

Prejudice means for one to have an idea about a person, place, or thing they believe to be the highest level of truth, even though it was formed without any firsthand experience, objective thought, or deep study. Prejudice is the mother of fear, and the friend of gossip, misunderstanding, and pride.

When one is prejudice against anything, they are unable to see it as it really is. It does not matter if the object is a thing, a being, or the whole of life itself. When someone mistakes wrong beliefs for right knowledge, that person takes inappropriate actions and choices that lead to more of the same.

In our world, there is a great deal of false information, stereotyping, and generalization. Because of this, we trust people we should not trust, fear things we should not fear, and feel strongly about what doesn't matter at all. Prejudice creates idiocy, and causes our political, religious, philosophical, and scientific systems of understanding to be infested with bias, opinion, and ignorance.

People think they *know* about everyone and everything, and the result is hardly anyone understands anything at all. Prejudice has taken the place of reason, and locked us into our cultures, sub-cultures, and personal illusions. Thus locked away, we have no interaction with information from other points of view, or with people from other cultures. Thus, we remain in a perpetual state of ignorance and error. We are stupid not because we lack intelligence, but because we think we already know. So how can we break the habit of protecting our biases and bad habits with ignorance? The answer is reason.

Reason is unemotional thinking about any person, place, or thing. It objectively studies all available information and follows the evidence no matter where it may lead. The mind guided by reason does not accept anything based upon one person's opinion, nor does it seek to protect the ideas it already has. Reason leads us to check all things we are told and think, against all available information. In this way, it frees us from tiny boxes and the agendas of others.

Prejudice causes us to see things from a very personal, local, and biased point of view. On the other hand, reason expands our mind, allowing us to see things from an impersonal, global, and unbiased point of view. The mind determined to be reasonable in all things, is a mind not carried away by misunderstanding or rash decisions.

The highest level of reasoning understands the limits of reason. Reason picks apart everything and puts it back together. It travels from point to point as the alphabet moves from letter to letter, and is powered by wisdom and knowledge.

Since reason deals in fact, if what is said to be a fact is really an error, reason cannot produce accurate results. Reason can only travel from point to point. If the starting point is unknown, or a middle step hidden, the conclusions reached by reasoning will be incorrect. Also, reason draws its power from the capacity and content of the mind using it. If the mind is ignorant, biased, or misinformed, accurate reasoning will lead to wrong conclusions.

The ability to accept the limits of knowledge is an attribute not possessed by those who are informed by prejudice. The biased mind does not need external evidence, clear demonstrations, or deep pools of supporting data. Thus, it can cling to whatever it believes or hopes to be knowledge without ever concerning itself with truth.

Prejudice prevents communication, personal growth, and the free flow of compassion and knowledge. It convinces people they are right without proof, shows others guilty without evidence, and makes the ignorance in the one possessing it incurable. Prejudice makes the mind a fort that will only let in the ideas of those who built it. Whatever culture the prejudiced mind was born into, there it will remain forever. It cannot free itself from its cultural ideas of right and wrong, even if they are incorrect, because it lacks the courage to doubt them.

Reason encourages communication, because it always looks into the unknown and seeks the deepest truth. Reason aids personal growth by correcting old ideas and teaching new ones. Most importantly, it lets us understand the circumstances and motives of others causing us to see our common humanity. Reason demonstrates what it says with proof, avoids generalizations, and rejects stereotypes. Reason is the friend of betterment, patience, humility, and truth. Thus, reason should be the friend of all who seek these things.

Pride and Humility

Pride is what we call the state of mind found in those who think themselves to be more important than they really are. Pride is the cohort of ignorance, prejudice, grudging, and cruelty; it is not at all to be confused with self-esteem. Self-esteem is based upon the actual value of one's self and the abilities they truly possess. It is a healthy awareness of one's personal potential, weakness, and uniqueness. Pride on the other hand, is based on how one perceives themselves, and the quality of their abilities when compared to others. It is an unhealthy forgetfulness of one's limits and mortality.

Those who are full of pride usually possess a high degree of skill, beauty, or merit, but they have allowed this to make them think too highly of themselves. This is illustrated well by the beautiful male peacock. It struts around trying to win the affections or respect of other peacocks with the qualities it possesses.

When we are full of pride, we are full of self. Our needs, wants, and ambitions cause us to be blind to less fortunate people. They are not seen as equals needing instruction or aid, but as inferiors. Thus, rather than having compassion the prideful mock, rather than noticing they pass by, and rather than applying their resources to help others they use them for self-betterment.

Pride makes the ignorant remarks of a stranger into a personal attack, so proud people are pulled into many unnecessary quarrels. Pride turns wise advice into silly comments not to be regarded, so the prideful remain in an ignorance that cannot be corrected. Pride also turns us into the slaves of other people. The mind becomes so filled with flattery, praise, and reputation it does not realize these things are controlling it. Just as a monkey dances to its masters beat to get a treat, so do the prideful dance to the rhythm of their peer group's praise.

Those who are full of themselves, destroy themselves with their own behavior. Gloating about their intellect they fail to see their ignorance, and end up suffering many unpleasant consequences due to their wrong actions and ideas. Showcasing their riches, they attract thieves who rob them in the dark with a mask, and in the daytime with a smile. Talking about their might and power, they attract rivals with superior skill who best them. Thus, their illusion bursts and their will deflates.

Another flaw of pride is the difficulty it adds to recovering from failure. All of us fail, and in every failure there is some sense of disappointment, even if it just passes through us. When those close to the ground fall, their breaks are not bad and so they mend quickly. Any lessons contained in the failure are received and applied rapidly. This is not the case with those who have pride. They have put themselves atop a high tower and when it topples, and it will topple, they hit the ground much harder. Hopefully, they have some real friends because once they fall the masses will turn on them.

What the public adores is success, power, and beauty. They love these things, because they lack the heredity or the will to gain personal possession of them. Therefore, they live out their dreams through their idols and icons. However, the public who praises and makes one wealthy, will also devour and make poor those who no longer feed their fantasies. The army of wolves that gave them power, rend them to pieces when they start to bleed.

The alternative to pride is humility, or the absence of wrong ideas about our self and others. Humility is the associate of wisdom, honesty, and forgiveness. True humility is not making oneself into a mud hole for people to walk through, it is the ability to acknowledge our flaws, admit our strengths, and bravely defend our rights.

Humility comes from accepting yourself, others, and reality just the way they are. When one understands the beauty of life, the potential of humanity, and the limitations of our kind, a teachable and deep mind is produced.

The humble minded are made up of people varying in strength, intellect, wealth, and physical beauty. These have seen their smallness and the problems in the world, and become empty of wrong ideas about themselves and all around them. Thus emptied, they see all beings as they are, and look upon the potential and value of others rather than their physical appearance. To those who have suffered misfortune they give love, as they pass by those with need they give notice, and they use their resources to help others as much as possible. The humble in spirit are the true kings of the earth, and wise virtue more splendid than the decorations of royalty.

Since the humble do not have a personal image to maintain, they let the rude comments of others pass by and avoid many useless conflicts. Their mind is teachable, so insight and understanding flow easily into them. The humble are quick to listen, and because of it they learn from the mistakes of others, not having to suffer the consequences of personal error in order to obtain understanding. The humble are freed from the opinions and esteem of others, because they do not have a reputation or image to protect. They live in total freedom.

Just as the prideful generate their own suffering and demise, so the actions of the humble bring them greatness and prosperity. Realizing their lack of understanding, they seek wisdom and learn how to act rightly, thus avoiding many miseries. The humble know what is most valuable cannot be seen, and so do not flaunt their material accomplishments. This prevents them from attracting the attention of thieves and parasites.

Speaking only what needs to be said, or what will give joy, they attract friends of high quality and provoke none. Even if they are wounded for speaking truth, or because their right actions have revealed the wrong motives of another, they are not ashamed or sad; they suffer for their kindness and not their cruelty. When the humble fall they do not fall far. Looking up from the ground they do not see a pack of wolves ready to consume them, but the friends their kind and unassuming manner has won.

Justice and Injustice

To be just means to be guided by honesty, instructed by reason, to honor truth above everything, and to care equally for the needs of all living things. Justice is the word we use to describe how a just person interacts with themselves, others, and situations. Injustice then is to deal with one's self, others, or a circumstance in a way that is dishonest, illogical, and prejudiced.

When one is not just in their dealings with other humans, they are begging to be hated, harmed, defamed, or killed. These effects are bad enough, but when you think about how unjust actions affect others it gets much worse. People who need help are denied and so continue to suffer, people who need truth are denied and so fall more deeply into despair, and people who have invested their time, talents, and resources are refused payment.

The greater the influence one has on others, the more harm is done when that individual behaves in an unjust way. When a peasant acts unjustly, children are misguided and neighbors are mistreated. They become renowned for being unkind, thus making themselves the target for the unkindness of others. However, when those who have power, wealth, or influence behave unjustly, the amount of harm caused is much greater.

When people in the legal system behave unjustly, they produce some of the worst outcomes. The innocent are made to suffer by the selfishness of those who are supposed to be serving and protecting them. Once the law has failed to give assistance, or recompense them for their losses, the innocent not only suffer, but are tempted to live unjustly themselves. Not only are the innocent treated unfairly, but the guilty go unpunished, and so continue to harm their own life and the lives of others. Again, the greater the influence and fearlessness of the criminal, greater is the wake of destruction left behind when they fail to receive justice.

As horrible as the consequences of unjust law enforcement are, this misuse of power is not the worst. Those who do the most harm by behaving unjustly are those who have been entrusted with teaching humanity about reality, themselves, their origins, and their future.

Teachers, scientists, parents, and spiritual guides of all persuasions have the most sacred of duties. When the minds in these fields are corrupt, the impact it has is comparable to the moon smashing into earth, and the effects are just as horrifying. These drunken guides bias the minds of those they instruct, giving them ignorance in place of wisdom, evil in place of good, and illusion in place of truth. Failing to show what true control of mind and matter are, their hypocrisy causes the beauty and power of the truths they represent to be doubted, scorned, and hated. Instructors hold in their hands the future of those they instruct, and the future of our world. If their hands are full of injustice, suffering and lies is the only thing we should expect tomorrow to bring.

Now, compare this to the life of those who are just and true. By being fair and upright in all dealings with others, they in turn are treated justly, and come to be valued for their integrity. Those around them are given what they rightly deserve, those who need strength are empowered, and those who have given their resources are compensated appropriately for their investments. The just live a higher quality life, and improve the quality of life for every being around them.

Just as the effects of injustice grow with the rank and power of its host, so do the effects of justice. If the lowly are fair in all their transactions with others, families and towns prosper and flourish. When the rich, wise, and powerful act justly the people copy them. Their nation prospers, and through the example of their nation the world is made better.

When the legal systems are fair the corrupt are punished, their power is dissolved, and other criminals fear and cease their unlawful actions. When the doctors and researches of health are fair and honest, the sick keep their life and have enough money left to live it. When teachers are upright their students are taught equally, subjects are presented without bias, and because of this pupils learn how to think instead of what to think. There are no teacher's pets to earn exclusive privileges, neither are students neglected because they are slow, different, or loud.

Then, there are the employers. When they are fair and honest the employees are free in their thoughts, enjoy their labor, and are rewarded appropriately for it. In this way, the employer and the employee are made wealthier. Finally, when the preachers, sages, and professors are honest and just, they do not disgrace the tenets they teach. This generates interest in their philosophies, the practice of them grows, and the world is made a better place.

Lies and Truth

Lying is a simple perversion of the truth in order to make someone believe reality is different than it really is. Lies are the friend of desire, greed, and injustice.

Every word or action we take influences the life of another person in some way. Words and deeds create the foundation understanding and belief is built upon, and from which actions flow. When words and deeds are false, the person we are influencing with them is infected with false understandings and representations. This is like trying to build a house on top of cardboard painted to look like concrete. Though it will hold a little weight, at some point the structure will collapse, causing great and unavoidable misery.

A simple illustration of this is found in the kindness a wife shows her husband. If I tell my wife I enjoy the dish she made when I do not, she will continue to make it and I, in order to convince her of my lie, must continue to eat it. In reality, I hate the flavor of the dish and eventually become deeply unhappy with the fact I have to constantly eat it. This unhappiness will never remain hidden. It will surface in one aspect of my life or another, and whenever it does it will disrupt the harmony of the moment.

The longer I lie about liking the dish the more I have to eat it, the more I eat it the more unhappy I become, the more unhappy I am the stronger my inner tensions become, and great stress disrupts all areas of life. If the truth does not come out, this cycle will endlessly repeat. I will lie again and again in order to keep the truth hidden, and my tension will not only remain but deepen, disrupting my life even further.

However, a lie usually does not remain hidden. The facts about the raspberry dumplings will come out, and when they do my wife's feelings will be hurt. Every time she meant to be sweet and fix me a tasty dish, she was in fact causing me to suffer, and this makes her sad. However, sadness is not the only reaction; there are also feelings of betrayal, anger, and resentment.

Thus, even in such a simple thing as cookery one can see how a lie creates nothing but inconvenience and suffering. If I were to tell my wife up front the dumplings were not very good in a nice way, she would understand and either not cook them for me or change the recipe. By lying, I created undue stress for myself, put myself through fifty bad meals, and in the end still had to tell my wife the truth.

Lying at first creates harmony but in the end explodes into chaos, unlike truth which creates disharmony at first but in the end blooms into peace.

The greater the importance of the information, the more harm is caused by lying about it. "Where have you been son?" a concerned father asks. "I have been hiking in the woods", the son replies. Really the son was playing in an abandoned coal mine his dad had told him never to go into, and because he has lied a dangerous and harmful behavior is uncorrected. Sure, he will get into trouble if he tells the truth, but if he doesn't he could hurt himself badly or cause another who seeks to share the experience with him harm.

If the son manages to escape harm in the coal mine, and his dad never finds outs he went there, this is even worse. Now lying has become a good option in the young man's mind. He has learned lying not only can it get us things we would normally not be able to obtain, but it also keeps us from having to pay the price for receiving them. However, the day of reckoning always comes, and when it does the liar is exposed. Then, not only do they have to pay for what they have done, they also lose the trust of others.

Lying makes it possible to avoid taking responsibility for our actions, but until we choose to take responsibility we will never be happy. Humans always seek to blame another person, fate, or a spiritual force for their circumstances. However, the truth is we have made our circumstances, and the mind we use to deal with them by our choices. Until this is realized, we will not see the need to change what we do. As long as our actions are out of harmony with the way reality really works we will never be happy.

Lies are just shortcuts, ways of accomplishing a goal without doing any of the work. We want the praise of others, and so we lie to get it. This may get us what we want, but because we know we are lying we lose a level of peace, and experience only part of the joy we could have had. Likewise, we may cheat and lie to pass a test or get a job, but what have we gained? We have only cheated ourselves out of the knowledge exams and employers look for. Then, when the time comes to use the knowledge we are supposed to have, our lack and lies will be revealed.

The harm a lie does is based on the topic of the lie, how greatly it alters people's understanding, and how many people are influenced by it. For example, let's say a defense attorney lies for his client who has molested children. The lies of the attorney secure a verdict of not guilty, and his client is set free. However, rather than using this second chance to change his actions, the client learns from his mistakes and creates smarter plans. He commits fresh crimes executed so well law enforcement cannot catch him. How much harm and disorder do you think such an act would cause? The attorney was supposed to be a tool of justice hired to defend human rights, but by lying he unleashed a flood of injustice.

Lying also dissolves trust between people, and trust is the root from which compassion and understanding grow. Two people who do not trust each other can never have a complete relationship. Their actions will always be half-minded. Each of them are too busy allowing themselves a way out, watching their back, or trying to figure out what the other person is doing to create any real friendship.

Once trust is broken, it is very hard to mend. When you get the reputation for lying, people begin to disregard every word coming out of your mouth. I have friends I know are full of lies, and though I still love them, I consider what comes out of their mouth to be entertainment until I can verify it. Once a person has lied for years, it is hard to undo the harm caused by their lies. However, it is possible to do if they will seek forgiveness, and demonstrate the habit of dishonesty has been broken.

Even though all lies can be forgiven, sometimes trust has been violated so deeply it can never be repaired. For example, suppose I tell my lover I am a virgin when I am not, and we end up getting married. Two months after our wedding a sexually transmitted infection surfaces that I did not know I had. My partner knows she is not the source of it, because she really was a virgin before our wedding night. How do you think my lie is going to affect our relationship?

Another example is a daughter who breaks into her parent's home, and robs them of their valuables. She plays the role of concerned daughter flawlessly for years, and then one day her parents discover the truth. Can you imagine how her lie will affect the relationship she has with her parents?

Whenever someone is caught lying, all their former and future words and actions are called into question. If you lied to me and cried to prove your honesty, how many other times have your tears been false? If you lied to me and faked compassion to make it convincing, how many other times has your compassion been a fraud?

Lies are worthless things that do nothing but generate pain, distrust, blame, irresponsibility, guilt, and conflict. Those who insist upon lying are hurting themselves as much as others. They rob themselves of peace, self-respect, and the satisfaction of getting an honestly earned reward.

Truth is to lies as light is to darkness. In the dark people wander around unsure of what is really there. Upon the blackness, shadows play and trick the mind to fear, while any steps taken lead us into holes, walls, and other harmful obstacles. In the light, people can know where they are and see what is really there. In the light, shadows flee and the mind is freed from useless and intangible fears. People can see where they are going and walk the path without harming themselves or others.

To speak truth is to define something exactly the way it is. Truth is the friend of humility, wisdom, contentment, and prosperity.

To lie is easy and to speak the truth is hard. We must work tirelessly in order to find truth, and finding it means we must face the facts about our world and ourselves. As hard as it is to find, speak, and face, truth is still the key to freedom, and the only thing that can better our world.

When nothing but the truth is spoken, the person you are speaking to is given a factual base of information to build their lives on. This is like a carpenter who sells good wood. The person who buys his lumber can construct a house to withstand the harsh elements of reality; one that does not collapse when it is needed the most.

The truth lets us live in harmony with the way things really are, and being in harmony with reality is the secret to a joyful life. Going back to the illustration of a wife cooking her husband dinner, if he lets his wife know as soon as she makes the dish he does not like it then he does not have to eat anymore bad food. Also, he and his wife are made closer through communication. By communicating she learns more of him, he learns more of her, and through this knowledge they learn to love each other for who they are. Thus, being truthful accomplishes what lying is supposed to do, while lies by their very nature rob us of our desires.

Being honest and upfront prevents us from being pulled into all the anxieties and complications created by lying. I do not have to remember what lie I told to whom or the details of my lies. Neither, do I worry about being caught in a lie, thus avoiding a permanent state of unrest. The honest take actions leading to reward and self-respect, rather than to punishment and shame.

By always telling the truth to ourselves and others, we never fail to see our mistakes, never fail to accept them, and never fail at learning how to make ourselves better. When we tell the truth and operate truthfully, we earn the praise, possessions, rank, power, and peace we desired, and can enjoy them because we are free of guilt. Also, when we are tried by the fires of circumstance they will reveal our strength and skill, rather than our lies.

Truth is the key to happiness because it teaches us the way things really are so we can know how to act. By right action we get right effects, and since we have obtained them rightly, there are no shadows cast upon our joy.

Truth binds people together. When one gains a reputation for always being truthful people trust them. Trust leads to communication, communication leads to understanding, and by understanding each other we obtain harmony. When we are truthful, people do not need to watch their back, and so enjoy their moments with us without any reservations. This allows all to have great experiences and create pleasant memories. Since others are able to trust us with all they have, they do not withhold themselves or their resources. This makes large tasks easier to accomplish and partnerships to prosper. Those who would accomplish truly great things must first be truthful.

Truthful people are also motivated to live rightly and kindly. The reason being, if they do wrong they know they must accept responsibility for it. Knowing all they do will come to light, they make it a point to do all things purely and well. By doing all things purely and well, they gain the trust and friendship of others. Producing quality work and obtaining quality friends, they are carried to places of joy and fulfillment. In this way, truthful people get the things they desire, and retain all relationships they have made. This may seem unimportant, but should they lose their riches or power, they will still possess still greater treasures - inner peace and true friends.

Abuse and Proper Use

Everything in the Universe has a use, and it is the function of wisdom to not only find out how things should be used, but to ensure they are not abused.

Abuse here means to use something in a way that is harmful to life. It is the brother of craving and friends with greed, ignorance, and sloth. It does not matter if it is an element of the material or mental world, everything can be abused. Whenever we abuse something we are misusing it, and when things are misused they decay, become misshapen, and lose their ability to function.

Whenever the body is abused it loses proper shape and organs function below their potentials. If the abuse is continued over time, the body is made ill. Like a car that isn't cared for properly the parts break down, the vehicle becomes useless, and the driver becomes very unhappy.

Just as we have divided reality, so we have done with ourselves. In our day, we no longer see mind and body as one, but in truth they are undivided. Those who misuse the body harm the mind, and those who harm the mind harm the body. There is not a single degree of separation between them.

It is easy for humans to forsake self-control, because ease is always preferable to difficulty. As this happens, the indulgences of one generation become those of the next, and the perversions of nature committed by those around us become ours.

Those who sell goods and services know this. Every moment we have our minds bombarded with images, words, and sounds intended to make us to crave something. Food, drinks, cloths, cars, and even other human beings are marketed in ways to awaken desire and prompt action. No wonder so many people in the world are suffering.

We abuse the pleasures of sex, food, and drink, abuse the understanding given by wisdom, knowledge, and reason, and destroy our earth, water, and sky by misuse. All of these abuses destroy the benefits found in the items being used, as well harming the one misusing them.

Abuse of our world has polluted our waters, scarred our skies, and wounded the earth. Through the abuse of wisdom, knowledge, and reason selfish hypocrites get rich at the expense of others, illnesses go uncured, and those who would have otherwise lived purely are corrupted. Chemicals that would be beneficial if used rightly, we make into a curse. Meanwhile, abuses of food, sex, and drink have weakened our minds, sickened our bodies, and rotted our wills. This miserable state of affairs needs to be changed, not by religious force or civil laws, but by all of us making the choice to become wise and to use everything wisely.

Everything in the universe has a function and a role it fulfills. If we will make the effort to become wise, to understand how our bodies, minds, and world work, we can know the nature and effects of each thing. Thus, we can use them properly.

Proper use means to use the needed amount of the right thing in the right way. The *needed* part is very important, because the human tendency is to mistake desire for need. Thus, we do not stop at enough, neither do we accept the best - we must have more and it must be better. This causes us to be perpetually tired, fearful of loss, and forgetful of the things that matter most in life.

When we seek to have enough and accept the outcome of our best efforts, when we meet our needs and then rest, and when we use things as they are meant to be used, then we are living lives that brim with fulfillment and wellness.

The way a thing is meant to be used and its needs are built into the thing itself. When we build cars, we also build into them the need for oil, water, gas, and a driver to guide and maintain them. Just like cars, everything in the natural world has its needs built in. Trees need sun, water, air, and soil because these things power the processes within them, and provide the materials and energy needed for growth. Cats, spiders, whales, seeds, and everything else is put together in a certain way, sustained in a certain way, and passes out of existence in a certain way.

If humans would begin to use sex properly the amount of us who are ill, without parents, or heart broke would drastically decrease. If we would use food and drink correctly death rates would fall, illnesses would decrease, and fewer would be misshapen and depressed. Our resources could be devoted to improving ourselves and our world, rather than fixing them. If we would correctly use chemicals they could serve and better our minds and bodies, rather than deteriorate them.

Likewise, if we would use wisdom, knowledge, and reason correctly we could find cures for those who are now ill, answers for the problems our abuses have caused, and insights into mysteries we cannot now fathom.

If only we could see whatever we do to the earth we do to ourselves. If we kill our planet we are doomed to share its fate. We need to watch nature, learn how the earth works, and then harmonize our actions with the natural flow. This would heal our land, clear our skies, and restore purity to our waters. We must start to use our sky correctly, because it contains the air we breathe, and protects us from rays and rock that would otherwise do us harm. We must start to use our water correctly, because it is the rivers and oceans powering our food, the clouds fueling our crops, and the liquid refreshing our children. We must also stop abusing our land, because it forms our food, filters our water, and gives us the space we need to live.

What is used well treats others well. Just as a well-cared for body gives strength to the life it creates, so a well- cared for earth will give health and sustenance to all it contains. If we continue to mistreat it, then the changes we have made to its systems will lead to the extinction of all living things. Proper use is not the only course of action open to us, but it is the only one that will take to wellness and life.

Apathy and Compassion

When one does not care, it is the mental substance called apathy. Apathy is the state of being empty of feelings, consideration, or concern for others. It is the friend of indulgence, ignorance, and greed.

Hate is an awful thing. It robs the mind of its ability to think rightly, to see clearly, to forgive wholly, and to act correctly. Much of the sorrow and destruction in our earth can be traced back to this element of error. However, all the harm hate actively causes is silently mirrored by apathy.

In order for error to rule the earth it does not have to be better or stronger than truth, it only needs more people acting on its behalf. When people do not devote themselves to good or evil, they may think they are being neutral, but doing nothing is not comparable to being neutral. If we do nothing, our failure to act becomes the action we have chosen to take. We are not doing harm directly, but there is much harm brought to pass as a direct result of our apathy. When you add those who are doing nothing and those who are doing evil, error outnumbers truth two to one.

All things in the universe have their place, and when they fail to fulfill their role, or behave in the proper way, the result is disorder, breakdown, and death. By this point, it is clear the best thing on earth for the human organism is to be devoted to right thought and right action. Whenever a human does nothing, they are not fulfilling their role in the earth. Just as a malfunctioning cell leads to a malfunctioning body, so do those who fail to make the earth healthy contribute to the decay and destruction of all it contains.

Apathy is like a benign tumor that never stops growing. It is not destructive like cancer, but it crowds the other parts and prevents them from working as they should. If humanity were a woman with child walking through a snow storm, apathy would be the car that drove by. Not caring is among the greatest of crimes, not because it acts incorrectly, but because it does not act at all.

The only cure for this horrible state of affairs is compassion. When we look upon one who is suffering, understand their situation, and feel their pain as though it was ours, then we are compassionate. Compassion is wisdom's sister, truth's purpose, and the companion of kindness.

Why do I say compassion and not love? Love has become a weak word. We love our cars, our dogs, our jobs, our shirt, our bed, and a million other mundane things. Also, love can mean anything from sexual desire to parental concern. Compassion on the other hand has not been overused, and is not as prone to misunderstanding.

Compassion if one of the greatest forces humanity has ever seen. If I am living for myself, I am ten times weaker than the one who lives to better those around them. When I am wounded and my world begins to crumble, if my motives go no deeper than self-advancement I am more inclined to surrender to weakness and despair. However, if my motive is the betterment of the world, then all the hurts of life cannot stop me. I see the harm my inactivity would cause others, and since their life is as valuable as mine I strive on, because I do not want them to feel the pain I now endure.

Our world is like a desert expanse where the water of compassion is becoming harder and harder to find. It seems humans no longer care only because they are kind. Now they care because they seek to obtain rewards, to avoid punishments, or to have others think highly of them. The mind that spontaneously pours out compassion without a thought, without a motive, and without a moral or legal code prompting them to action is like an oasis. Those who come into contact with them have their mind refreshed. Having tasted pure compassion, others will fall in love with it, become filled with it, and in turn be made into an oasis of compassion themselves. If all people would become devoted to truth and compassion, this cycle would repeat until our dry world was like a watered garden.

Compassion acts, heals, and strengthens those who are hurting until their pain disappears, or they have the strength to bear it. Apathy on the other hand, simply stands and watches the harmful energies and circumstances of life devour and sicken everything.

Measurement Results

Having looked at how the different forms of truth and error affect their host and world, it is obvious what actions and thoughts are in harmony with human existence. To allow evil and error to fill and run your life causes decay and malfunction. Evil harms those animated by it spiritually, psychologically, and materially.

Error is the reason for all human suffering. It is the lust seeking to take the homeland of another, the pride refusing to seek equality and peace, the unforgiving mind dedicating a nation to acts of endless vengeance, the abuses of the wealthy forcing the poor to steal just to survive, and all the other forms evil takes. All war, crime, and injustice would fade into nonexistence if error in all its forms were cast out of the minds of humanity.

Those who equate light and dark with good and evil are forgetting the limits of metaphor. Evil is not darkness although it blinds the mind, and goodness it not light even though it enlightens. When light shines upon something it creates shadow, but what evil is done by a mind filled with goodness?

Evil does at times come from others when purity makes them aware of their shortcomings. Also, to dedicate time to one good deed prevents us from simultaneously doing another. However, the first is a product of the evil in the mind of another, and the second is a consequence of being a creature bound by space and time.

If all humanity sought, thought, and expressed truth exclusively, only goodness would exist. The only reason why it is impossible to end evil is because so many people love themselves and their ideas too much to change. Selfishness is the father of all error. When we love ourselves more than others, we are like the heart that hops out of the body so it can do what it wants. By doing this it kills itself and the body as well. As long as humanity is full of the illusion individuals can prosper at the expense of the global community, things will continue as they are until the world ends, or we drive ourselves to extinction.

Selfishness causes us to view ourselves as wholes when in reality we are only parts. As long as we see ourselves as separate and different from others, it is impossible for compassion or any other form of truth to thrive. Such a state of separation now exists. This is why so little goodness and truth gets beyond the walls of our cultural and sub-cultural groups.

We have divided ourselves into nations, states, and cities. Then we divide ourselves into even smaller groups based on the way we talk, the way we dress, the color of our skin, the type of music we like, the amount of money we make, or any number of other superficial divisions. We put ourselves into tiny little boxes with great big walls, and see all who are on the outside as different or less than we are.

As if the division of our earth and ourselves were not enough, we have also divided the truth into small segments. Then, we set about trying to use one part of truth to prove another part is wrong. It like a physicist, a biologist, a farmer, and a cook arguing over who knows the ultimate truth of apple trees. The physicist understands how the atoms work, and scoffs at the cook for his ignorance about the atomic world. The biologist scoffs at the physicist, because he hasn't dedicated enough time studying how atoms translate into living things. The cook thinks both the biologist and the physicist are foolish, because neither of them have any idea how to use apples in a practical way. Meanwhile, the farmer thinks they all have something to learn, because without him they would not have an apple tree to argue about.

They are all right in what they know, they all have something to learn, and they all have something to teach. However, if they only look at their differences, they will never grow wiser or glimpse the unity of their knowledge.

In the same way, members of one religion see themselves as the only teachers of truth, and all other religions as fools who need to learn. One religion will call themselves the saints, and label all who do not think like they do lost, evil, or inferior. Whenever we get these wrong views in our head, they cause us to distrust and prejudge others. This causes misunderstanding, and then we commit acts of injustice and evil against people who are innocent and pure. Do not think for a moment this type of thinking is limited to the religious realm, it applies equally to the realm of politics, science, and color of skin.

We have divided everything and every idea in the universe into a billion pieces, and then wonder why nothing fits together. By our own assumptions, pride, ignorance, and selfishness we have prevented our race from understanding the universe correctly and realizing our place in it.

The amount of error in our world has become so great only an apocalypse can purge it, but the apocalypse does not have to come from the outside. If each and every human would rid themselves of wrong thought and action, if each of us had our own personal Armageddon on the inside, then this whole world could change for the better. If all were dedicated to truth, it would not matter how much error inducing information existed in the world. It would be so contrary to our nature we would just ignore it, as a honey bee ignores a stack of crap on its way to the flower. Truth would be the theme of every mind and by the continual practice of goodness evil would eventually be flushed from the human experience. However, in order for this to happen, each and every human on earth has to purge themselves and make truth the motive of all their actions. The change from truth to error has to come from within, if it is imposed from without the only result will be rebellion.

Even if we cannot flush evil from the earth, we can at least flush it from our individual selves. We do this by making truth the central principle of our existence. Just as selfishness is the root of all evil, so selflessness is the base of all goodness.

Selflessness does not mean neglecting one's own need it simply means the needs of everyone else are *just* as important as our own. Those who have truly grasped this, is a spring of goodness refreshing itself and all who drink from it.

If selfishness is like the heart that left its body to try to make its own way, then selflessness is a body where all the parts realize their fates are interwoven. If one succeeds then all succeed, and if one fails all fail. This is the way all reality is built. Without roots the whole tree cannot grow, if one link in a chain fails the whole thing is broken, and if one part of the body aches all parts react to its pain.

Everywhere you look in the material world, the lesson of unity and interdependence is being taught. The question is will we learn, or will we blunder on in the errors that have brought us to the place in human history we are today. For thousands of years, we have put forth a continued and determined effort to deepen our divisions and emphasize our differences. This has only brought war, slavery, injustice, and poverty. We need to unify before we die, and there is only one way to do this - we must wipe the slate clean and start over.

Letting go of everything our society has told us about what we are, where we are from, and what reality is, we will then be free to build a world without evil and without walls. If we will let go of the wrong ideas we have about ourselves, others, and our world, we can realize all of our potential and make the world anything we want it to be. The only impossible thing is the thing we think impossible.

Beyond All Walls

Young Man had learned a lot from Old Beauty. As he looked at the world through his new eyes, he saw how people killed each other in the name of life, how the crafty use the faith of the simple to manipulate them, and how the poor suffer at the hands of the greedy. His heart hurt and he deeply wanted to find a way to cure humanity of the needless misery it caused.

Young Man had almost given himself to despair when he remembered his friend who lived on the Mountain. He left to go see her, but the trip did not still his mind. All the way up the Mountain he thought of humanity's self- inflicted suffering, and by the time he got to the top he was in tears. As Young Man neared her tent, Old Beauty heard him weeping. Going to meet to him, she invited him in, made some relaxing peppermint tea, and asked what was weighing on his heart.

Young Man told Old Beauty the source of his perplexities and then asked, "Can humanity live in harmony with itself and the world around it, and if it can then how?" Old Beauty's heart went out to the suffering young man. Many times she had wept because of the ways evil and ignorant people had destroyed the earth and warped human society. Taking a moment to collect herself she placed one arm around her pupil as though he were her son and said, "Once there was a very wise sage who lived on a mountain something like mine. From the mountain top he looked down upon the civilized world beneath him, and marveled at the pain his brothers and sisters caused one another."

"The sage thought, 'I will teach them knowledge, lead them to wisdom, and instruct them in the way of Heaven.' However, every time he taught someone something, they thought themselves special and became proud. This pride led to conflicts. As war gripped human society, the sage watched his brothers and sisters use the knowledge he had given to craft fearful weapons of death. This saddened him and so he thought, 'I will show them the wonders of peace, the joy of compassion, and the way of kindness.' However, after he taught these things, people showed compassion only to those like them, gave kindness only when it was beneficial, and became peaceful only after all other options were exhausted."

"The sage was bewildered with grief and thought, 'How can I cause my brothers and sisters to see the beauty of living, how can I lead them to the bliss of virtuous unity?' He applied all his wisdom and created a machine like no other. This machine had the power to make each human see life from the perspective of all other things. The sage walked to the center of the earth and turned it on."

Instantly, each person looked through the eyes of the animals, and saw how greed had ruined their homes and poisoned their bodies. Everyone saw through the eyes of the earth how they were abusing her. They realized if they kept destroying the air, the water, and the land soon they would end all life on earth. However, most wondrous of all, they saw through the eyes of the poor, felt the pangs of the starving, and realized their enemies were only mirror images of themselves. The earth was illumined with an understanding of the oneness of all living things."

"The next day some wanted to kill the sage for showing them their corruption, and some wanted to kill him for undermining their ideas of truth. Others thought the sage to be out of touch with reality and ignorant regarding the ancient prophecies. Though they agreed his vision was true, they thought it a waste of time. Then, there were those who realized Heaven did not determine their fate, it only predicted what would happen if they refused to walk the path of wisdom. They also saw the only thing limiting humanity was its beliefs about what is possible. They realized if each human would devote themselves to kindness and truth, earth and all life on it could heal."

"The sage watched from ground level all the actions he had produced in the minds of the people. He knew all too well how powerful men skew information and lie to bind the simple to their wills. He saw how religious leaders loved the power given to them by those who followed their traditions more than they loved the truth. Also, he knew how deeply attached to evil humanity had become."

"This knowledge would have crushed him were it not for three understandings. He knew truth to be the most powerful thing on earth. He understood evil was temporary, because in the end it destroys even itself. Best of all, he knew Heaven had put on earth all the wisdom and resources needed to accomplish anything. Returning to his mountain the sage took a seat, ate some rice, drank some tea, and thought, 'Will we choose purity and recreate our world by wisdom, or is Apocalypse indeed the only solution?'

Chapter Sixteen

We live in a time unlike any other in all of known history. No longer is humanity divided by expanses of water and land, because technology has made our planet a global community. Planes carry us from one side of the world to the other, satellites instantly beam news of foreign events to us, and the internet carries the events of life into the homes of billions.

Even though we are now unified in the realm of space and time, we are still deeply divided in our minds. For thousands of years humans lived in isolated pockets. In this isolation cultures formed, each with their own ideas of where we come from, how we should live, how government should be run, and where we are going after death. As time passed, each culture expanded on the ideas of its forefathers, producing volumes of books containing a unique understanding of life.

For thousands of years, these collections of writings and other sacred traditions were taught to the people in their area as the source of highest truth. These texts and rites have been obeyed as the voice of God, honored as the instructions for happiness, and turned to for comfort and answers in times of bewilderment and grief.

Eventually, each culture refined its ideas until their system was complete. People born into their culture were given an identity and a name by the people around them, taught how to speak and read words, told what questions they needed to ask, and then given answers to those questions. The end result was every human born into any social system had a complete understanding of itself, its world, its origin, and its future.

As human understanding and exploration increased, people began to encounter other humans who had identities, and systems of understanding, totally different than their own. Some were intrigued by this and took up the study of exotic wisdom. Others took no notice because they already had their answers. However, a third group did not like this intrusion of foreign ideas, and declared philosophical war against them. Some fought because these ideas made them doubt their personal identity, and the answers their teachers had given. Some fought because they saw these strange ideas as the work of evil powers trying to creep in and corrupt the obvious truth. Still others fought merely because someone told them too.

This war of ideas which began long ago lies at the heart of all the bloodshed now engulfing the globe. Each government on the face of the earth arose from a unique philosophical or religious system. These systems shaped their civil laws and personal identities. Almost every culture's system of wisdom tries to establish itself as being the most accurate expression of truth. Because of this, humans have been caught up in trying to establish the ideas of their culture as superior to all others ever since.

This is fine and even healthy as long as people conduct their warfare with logical argument, philosophical demonstration, and empirical evidence. However, many have forgone these beneficial forms of controversy. Instead, corrupt, misinformed, or fearful people have chosen to use force and civil law to establish the superiority of their thoughts and information.

When one attempts to use force and governmental power to rule the mind of another, they have stepped beyond their authority and forsaken the path of wisdom. Truth does not need force because it can demonstrate its claims, and the lives of those who embody it have virtue able to convince all doubters. Only when a system has lost its connection with wisdom, does it resort to external displays of wealth and power to persuade people of opposing views. What it cannot accomplish by reason and compassion, it tries to achieve with shame, peer pressure, isolation, glamor, and force. It does not realize by doing this, it is using error and evil in order to prove its accuracy and goodness.

Shame only forces the mind to comply with what it has been told. It does not give understanding, and so it is doomed to create only confusion and rebellion. Peer pressure is much the same. It keeps the individual's mind in a cage by saying, "If you think differently than me you will have no job, no friends, no family, and no hope of heaven". In this way, fear and punishment become the motive for faith and goodness. This corrupts the mind and causes people to become slaves, zealots, or outcasts.

Then there is isolation. Political, religious, and philosophical leaders use people's hopes and fears to make them believe there is only one source of truth on earth. Once the mind has been shut to all but one source of information, whoever controls the flow of information controls the mind. This is the way cults keep their followers, and how governments bind the minds of people to their political agendas. Even though the individual thinks their minds are free, in reality they have been led to every conclusion, and shaped into what some wise or zealous mind wants them to be.

Finally, there is force. This makes the mind conform to one people group's set of ideas by using pain, punishment, and fear. Force only changes the exterior of a person. The individual does not understand why good is good and wrong is wrong, and so does not obtain a personal experience with purity. The moment the risk of punishment is gone, the individual will behave in destructive ways, because it has no understanding of why it should be good.

I reject all these methods, because they instill the mind with fear and misinformation to manipulate it. Ignorance and fear can only create division and error. All of these methods use these things in one way or another. Therefore, they are part of the problem, and any solution they seem to give will last only a little while before coming to a violent end.

For years now, I have studied the traditions of wisdom handed down by sages, prophets, scientists, and philosophers to every culture on earth. I began as a sincere follower of Jesus. Through that experience I have been led to a place I am not sure anyone else has ever been, but which I am certain everyone needs to visit.

Time and again, I have had what I thought I knew about life washed away, and time again I have rebuilt my understanding, each time incorporating the new truths I have learned. I have read hundreds of books, and from each one I have learned a part of truth I did not know before. However, I have seen in all of them how the culture and perspective of the author has prevented them from seeing and grasping aspects of truth.

As I seen how culture, preference, and perspective affected each of the authors, I came to understand how it affected me. At first this thought terrified me. However, realizing ignoring a truth will not change it, I decided to seek out and experience what each culture on earth calls true. As I did this, I realized how my own culture had literally created me. The name I have, the way I see myself and the world, even my ideas about how all things came to be were products of my culture. All the answers I had, all of what I called truth, were not conclusions I had reached based on personal study and reflection. Rather, they were the thoughts of someone else I had mistook for my own.

The more I studied, the more I realized everything I saw, thought, and experienced was being filtered through the understanding my teachers had given me. Have you ever wondered why there are so many interpretations of the different holy books, and so many religions? It is because individuals see the writings through the understanding and information given them by their teachers. The mind that has been raised in a Baptist church, and taught by Baptist theologians, reads a Baptist Bible. Meanwhile, the mind that has been raised in a Methodist church, and taught by Methodist theologians, reads a Methodist Bible even though they both are reading the same book.

This filtering of reality can be understood by comparing it to colored glass placed over one's eyes. Every culture and sub-culture has their own color of glass they put over the eyes of those born into them. Thus, all of us see the same scene, except we look at it through the lens of our culture which colors it in a unique way.

As I thought still deeper about how culture programs us, I realized even though we all have been given different colored glass, we are all still looking at the same reality. Then it hit me with the force of a hurricane, "What would someone see if they refused to wear anyone's colored glass?" The answer of course is they would see reality as it really is, they could witness every moment without bias, and eventually they might glimpse ultimate truth. So this is what I have done, and the book you have just read is an expression of what I have seen. It is true from beginning to end, and not in a limited cultural sense, but in the ultimate sense. There are things I believe but this is not a book about believing - there are plenty of those - this is a book about knowing.

However, my book is still not complete, because I have not yet shown you the world without lenses. I have merely explained how it works, and led you step by step up the ladder of wisdom to the top of the walls those around you have enclosed you in. Now that we are at the top, I would like to show you the wall-less world. However, as much as I would like to show it to you I can only express it in words, which are reflections of my thoughts, which are them self reflections of reality. This means all my words are merely shadows of what is real. Yet, as limited as my words may be, they are a gate through which those who are brave can walk and enter into a deeper understanding of reality.

This brings up a point I cannot help but address before moving on - understanding cannot be transferred from person to person. I can give you information, I can explain how things work, but until you educate yourself, and test my words you will not have understanding. When I read a book, I am only gathering information, I am not getting knowledge. If I accept what an author says without proving it to be true or false, then I have an explanation I believe in, but I do not have knowledge. I do not know.

This is why the quest for ultimate truth has to be personal. No one can step in and give you the answers and there are no short cuts to realization. It is a long and hard road we each must take. There are billions of voices in our world, each declaring they have knowledge, but in reality most of them have belief. For every book wrote by a man with a degree supporting one point of view, I can find another man with the same degree supporting the opposing view. Likewise, for every prophet or sage saying life is one way, I can find another one who says it is not that way at all. All these authority figures are just a bunch of talking heads mouthing words and making assertions. If we do not individually seek out understanding and apply the truth we find, we will be misled. We will end up only listening to those who say words that support our preexisting ideas and give us comfort.

Truth is an objective reality that must be experienced subjectively. In other words, there really are ultimate truths that apply to all people in all ages, yet these truths have to be understood and experienced on a personal level. Water in the spring is great, but unless you drink it you will die, and no other can swallow the water for you. It is for this reason no one but me has the right, or even the ability, to determine what is best for me spiritually, mentally, or materially.

From where I stand, you may seem a fool who clearly understands nothing. However, you could be wise and I believe you to be a fool only because I am foolish. What seems the deepest and most heavenly truth I have ever known might in reality be the useless ramblings of a cult leader, the wit of a wicked being, or a system of illusion set up by my ancestors to comfort them in an uncertain reality. I do not have the right to force you to think like me, and I certainly do not have the right to enforce my views through civil law.

Even though I do not have the right to force you to think like me, if something you are doing seems unwise, or I think I have information that would improve your life, then I should speak out. By communicating with each other in reasonable, dispassionate, and polite ways, we all gain perspectives and information we did not have before. I cannot command you to abandon your ideas, and you cannot demand I abandon mine. Even if your ideas are best, it is still my fate, my life, and my choice. It does not matter if my actions and ideas conflict with your spiritual values or moral code. As long as they do not infringe upon your civil liberties, you do not have the right to force me to comply for reasons we have already discussed. Yet, enough about differences let us look at our commonality.

Over the Walls

As scientists have studied our universe, they have found all energy, space, and time burst into existence at a definite point in history. This event is called the *singularity,* and setting aside whether or not it was caused by a metaphysical force, let us consider an aspect of it often overlooked. Notice, it is not called the *duality,* or the *triality,* it is called the *singularity,* meaning from this event everything we now witness came into being. This means all of us, all we see, and all we enjoy was brought into being by the same cause. There are not two creation events. What created you created me.

This event is also what brought the atomic world into being, and the atom is the basic energetic building block of every material thing. Every element we use, every substance we consume, even our very selves, is made of atoms. Do you know how many styles of atomic construction there are? There is only one in this universe - a positive charged packet of energy is joined to a neutrally charged packet of energy, and these are orbited by a negatively charged packet of energy. Anti-matter too uses this same construction but the placement of the positive and negative energies are reversed.

A common atomic structure is found in every element. The only thing differing between them is the amount of energy packets used in their construction. It is similar to the way a little wood and a few nails make a dog house, but a lot of wood and many nails make a people house. All the material things we see differ in appearance, but share a common atomic construction and behavior.

To show how similar the elements are, all we have to do is compare mercury to gold. Gold has only one less proton in its center than mercury does. Yet, gold is solid, non-toxic, and golden in color while mercury is liquid, toxic, and silver. Even though the appearance of the substances in our world differ greatly, underneath it all they are very similar. Appearances are deceiving.

Atoms get together and form elements, these elements get together and form molecules, and molecules get together to form cells. Cells are the smallest building blocks of all living things, and just like the atomic world, they are all constructed according to the same basic design and function in very similar ways. All the plants you see on earth, as varied in appearance as they are, have more in common than they have different. Only a comparatively small number of cellular differences exist between a rose and a weed.

All plants dig into the earth, reach toward the sun, and gather water to continue life. Though they differ in form, they have the same basic construction, nature, and behaviors. Underneath all the apparent differences there is a deeper underlying similarity.

What is true of the cells that make plants is also true of the cells that make animals. In fact, there are more similarities than differences even between plant and animal cells. In the world of living creatures, there is as much apparent difference as there is in all the other categories we looked at. Yet again, underneath it all there is more similarity than difference. The same basic cellular design and function that causes a frog to grow, is the same as what causes you and me to grow. All of life's diversity is due to a comparatively small amount of genetic information.

Some look at this commonality, and believe it proves we came from a common ancestor that got together without any metaphysical help. Others look at this commonality, and believe it proves we came from a common metaphysical root. However, this is not about what we believe, it is about what we are no matter what we believe.

All of reality came from one source, and that source is responsible for the creation of our solar system. Here, one star warms the surface of one planet on which dwells one race, determined to drive itself into extinction because of all their *differences*. If I sat for a million years and tried to imagine a more ridiculous scenario, I would never succeed. We all dwell in the same reality, we are all governed by the same cosmic principles, we are all built from the same things, we all have the same needs, and we all have common hopes and fears. What we *believe* does not have the slightest effect on the construction of reality, or the construction of the things within it.

Our cultures are the products of changes that occurred over time due to our isolation from one another. All of our differences are learned behaviors, but our commonality is built into our very nature by the source of our creation. Over time humanity has crafted unique kingdoms and unique collections of books to explain our life, our world, and our reality. All of these traditions and kingdoms are important. However, more important is the need to realize they are all interpretations of one reality, and all parts of one truth. Since they are all parts, none of them are complete in themselves.

There is not one book or one body of knowledge on earth that can teach any of us the total truth. Each of them is a gate opening into a deeper understanding. To pit the wisdom of one culture's traditional system of understanding against another is a mistake. Each of them began at different places, is spoken in different words, and has become part of their people just as your culture's religious and philosophical views have become a part of you. Every human on earth has something to teach and something to learn.

We live in an infinite reality filled with an infinite amount of truth, and we all have an infinite amount of room to grow in our understanding. We must see the commonality we share with our world, with other living things, and with each other. Without commonality there is only selfishness, and without understanding there is only ignorance. If selfishness and ignorance are our guides, we will destroy ourselves, and it will no longer matter who is *right* and who is *wrong*.

Allow all people the freedom to think, live, and speak the way they want as long as they do not violate your liberties. By mutually seeking to find the total truth no matter what changes in belief or action it might require of us, we can create a world where virtue reigns, and every person can live according to the dictates of their own conscience. Reason and respect are the only way we can build a peaceful world. If we try to force our ideas and agendas, we will only create disunity and rebellion.

All of us have our ideas about how the world works, where we came from, where we are going, and how we should live while we are here. Yet, our ideas do not change reality. The truth about our function, our origin, our destiny, and the best way to live is the truth. It does not matter what we believe. Our beliefs alter how we view where we came from, and how we view where we are going. However, the way of truth is eternal and unaffected by our hopes, fears, or misunderstandings.

In all the religious and philosophical works I have ever read, freedom, justice, mercy, knowledge, wisdom, equality, peace, and self-control are honored and pointed to as the way to live. If at any time we forsake these basic truths in order to further our beliefs, we are foolish and errant. We should respect others no matter who they are, and respect their beliefs no matter what they may be. Above all we should honor all others' freedom of choice, even when they choose to err.

None have the right to force my will or decide my fate, be they priests, presidents, gods, or kings. Whatever awaits us beyond this reality, each of us will face alone. If there is a recompense for the deeds we have done, then each of us will be rewarded or punished according to the judgment of Heaven, and not according to the narrow and biased judgments of humans.

We have to awaken to the oneness of all things otherwise none of us will survive. We are killing our world, because we do not see its fate and ours are intertwined. We are killing each other, because we do not see our common humanity. All humans want freedom, beauty, peace and health. We all enter life the same way, and we all exit it in the same way. If we could all just see and accept our oneness, we could stop the injustices done against each other and our world.

Our loyalty should be to truth and goodness above all else - above our government, above our religious and philosophical ideas, above our families, and above our very lives. Only when the truth has become this important to us, will any of us truly live or purely experience living. Only when every individual purely and truly lives will wars end, poverty cease, and evil forever become a thing of the past.

Thank you reader for sharing the time you have with me, but I would dare to ask one more favor. Please consider this life deeply, seek to understand eternity, and give to others the compassion and freedom you wish to have. If you do this, and share this truth with others, we can spark a flame changing our world into one family inside one house. If all devoted themselves to truth right now, humanity could banish evil from the earth, and heal all the wounds inflicted on us by our world and mortality.

However, we must choose to make truth the priority as individuals. Never should we ever try to make this choice for others. If we do, we will create only injustice, error, and ignorance. Truth allows others the right to commit evil, and the freedom to choose slavery. Similarly, justice allows others the right to suffer the consequences of their wrongs. Those who use power, ignorance, guilt, and fear to manipulate the wills of others have never seen truth, and will not see it until they look through new eyes.

If we each shared our knowledge with everyone else, and everyone else shared their knowledge with us, we each would multiply our understanding of the world by a factor of six billion. Imagine how much humanity could do if we all acted as one mind and set aside our greed and ignorance. Our world would become a whole new place, and the future we would leave for those who came after us would be golden.

This present reality is all we undeniably know. What does or does not exist beyond it can seldom be known as we know gravity. Any knowledge of it will always be mixed with differing amounts of faith. This is another reason why no one should demand others to comply with their ideas of the origin of reality or what might come after. Instead, they should educate, discuss, reason, and persuade, always leaving the final choice in the hands of each individual.

The idea I have, based on my current level of understanding, is we will all one day have to face our life's record. At that time Heaven, however it really is, will be the judge of our eternal destiny. No mortal on earth determines my fate but me. No philosophy or religion has the authority to demand my compliance, and no government's power extends beyond the grave.

Governments have the right to enforce a certain amount of practical morality, but they do not have the right to enforce any level of spiritual duty. They can dictate my civil actions, but have no right to manipulate my opinions. When religion dictates political policy, then religious rules become a matter of national loyalty. Then, any dissent from the national religion is seen as treason, and punished as a civil offense. Whenever governments conduct themselves in this way, they are nothing but a group of people trying to convince the world of their ideas by force. This is because they lack the wisdom, virtue, and proof to do it otherwise. How I relate to any spiritual system has nothing to do with my civil obedience. Besides, most all religions teach a high level of morality, so most all religious people will comply with any reasonable civil code.

Since we are a democracy, it is very important we remember these things, as well as the rights of the minorities among us. Whenever the majority of a democracies' voting block becomes convinced of a certain religious or philosophical system, if the democracy is not careful, a religious dictatorship is just around the corner. In our world today, religious tensions run high, and without wisdom and communication these tensions will first divide and then destroy us.

I see in America a trend toward this division, and the possibility of the mainstream forms of Christianity using the power of their majority to put people supporting their faith into office. Then, through them they could put their spiritual ideas into civil law. I understand how distressing it is for people who love purity to see the immorality and greed now running rampant in our society, and I admire all who are devoted to improving the moral character of our nation. However, I cannot lend any support to the strong ties that have developed between religious elements in America and our civil government.

America was founded by a group of people who crossed the ocean so they could worship God according to the dictates of their conscience. They left a land where kings and popes had forced religious views on the people they ruled with treats of death and imprisonment if they did not conform. The founding fathers had experienced first-hand the injustices that take place when a single religious sect wields the sword of government. They sought to prevent this by putting in the constitution a clause that prevented the government from making any laws favoring *any* religious institution.

However, that was more than two hundred years ago. All who now live in America have never had to experience the pain of forced worship. It is for this reason so many are pushing law makers to fashion laws favoring their own religious views.

I have spent a lot of time reading the words of Jesus, and it is clear from what he said that he saw the dangers of church controlling state. In Matthew 22:17-21, Jesus says people should give to the government the things rightly belonging to the government and to God the things rightly belonging to God. Then again in John 18:33-36, when Pilate asked Jesus if he was a king, and said Jesus' nation had delivered him to be punished, Jesus replied his kingdom is not a worldly kingdom. He said his kingdom would be set up at a later date, referring to his second coming and the establishment of his rule on the earth at that time, as Matthew 13:36-43 makes clear. In fact, Jesus refused to serve in the capacity of a civil judge. In Luke 12:13-14, when he was asked to determine how an inheritance should be divided he asked the person why they were coming to him as though he were a judge of such matters. Jesus confessed to being the judge of human souls, John 5:21-23, but not of human property.

Those who seek to establish an earthly kingdom in the name of Jesus, are doing so in direct opposition to the clear example set forth by the founder of their religion. In fact, at one point in time a large part of the earth was governed by a power who professed to rule in the name of Jesus. Under the influence of papal rule, Europe experienced the darkest days of its history. Millions were put to death because they would not accept the government's interpretation of a human's duty to God, and mass ignorance became the rule of the day. Thus, if anyone should doubt Jesus knew what he was talking about when he separated the duty of people to their government from the duty of people to their God, history provides proof he was right.

If people want to preserve the purity of their children, and improve the spiritual character of our government, they need to do so by educating people about the joys of purity and the wisdom of virtue. It does not matter what our government does, it matters what we do in our homes. If people would teach the truth in their homes, and learn the art of controlling their minds rather than trying to control their environment, even if all the earth became filled with error the followers of truth could keep their minds unspotted at all times.

I understand there are many voices in our nation, and around the world, that have raised grave doubts about the validly of the Bible and the identity of Jesus. However, taking over the government and using force to keep them from speaking does not make their questions go away. In fact, it validates their doubts, because they see people who are supposed to be wise, loving, and kind resorting to the same methods used by secular governments to silence those who do not like their policies. I have read all sides of the argument, and each side has good points and bad points. It is not as clear as either side would like for it to be, and this lack of clarity shows neither side can prove their points as scientists can prove gravity. Again, a little faith is always involved. All matters pertaining to how a person relates to the idea of God should be decided on an individual level, and not on a national one.

It is the duty of political leaders in our nation not only to represent the majority that will keep them in office, but also the interests and rights of the minorities. We are a diverse nation made up of people from many cultures and many religious views. It is this diversity, and the freedom to be diverse, that has made America so great. If we force those who come to us seeking freedom to adopt our religious and national values, then we have become the very type of government our founding fathers sought to escape. Let us not silence the bell of liberty with the thunder of dogma, and the drums of misguided zeal.

Living in a land where there is freedom of speech means there are times when you will have your ideas challenged, and your peace disturbed. Yet, challenge breeds improvement and excellence. If we silence by force the voices that challenge us, we will decay and become mentally weak. By exposing myself to every point of view, I have been forced to become wise, deep, and knowledgeable. My life and understanding have improved a hundredfold, because I have honestly considered the ideas of others. If I had just stuck my head in a hole my life would be easier, but my mind would be narrow and filled with the ideas of those around me regardless if they were true. If you think someone is wrong challenge them and demonstrate your proofs. If they prove your ideas wrong then you have become better, and if they cannot you have bettered them.

How life began, how to live it, and the possibility of God are too big for any one person, one religion, one branch of knowledge, or one nation to answer. We need to come together and make our world a place where all have their needs met, so all can have the time to consider these deeper questions the way they should. We can no longer afford to assume all we think is right, and all the ideas of others are wrong. The issues are too important and the consequences of failure to dire for us to be narrow minded about these things. We need to have open minds and keep all of our options open. Let us not turn the question of human freedom and well being into a political game, where leaders manipulate trusting people by saying what they want to hear. Neither should we let people spin the information to make their side sound true, no matter what their side may be saying.

How much more suffering must we endure before we wake up? How many more lives must be lost fighting over pieces of dirt none of us can keep? How many more people must starve to death while we spend billions entertaining and indulging ourselves? How much of the earth must we destroy before we realize we are destroying the very thing our lives depend on? Wisdom, truth, unity, and peace are more important than our national, religious, and personal identities. We are all united on a cosmic scale, and our common humanity is written into our very nature. Let us then no longer allow the superficial bonds created by our human systems prevent us from honoring our natural bonds.

We are at a pivotal moment in the history of the earth, and it is time for us as global family to wake up and decide our fate. We are destroying our world with pollution, greed, and selfishness. Once it is gone, that is it. We are on the only speck of rock capable of sustaining life that we currently know of. Earth is an island in the middle of a cosmic ocean, and we are tearing it apart piece by piece. We are not going to get on a ship and zoom around space any time in the near future, and even if you think God is coming back to save us who knows how much longer that will be? If we do not alter our actions, we are going to destroy everything and create endless amounts of unnecessary suffering. This is not a philosophical, political, religious, or scientific issue. This is a human issue, and whether we live or die depends on us understanding this.

How shall we change? Shall we cast away everything we have been taught all of our lives in an instant, and come together in a moment of supreme oneness? It has taken thousands of years for us to become as divided and misguided as we are at this point, and it will take time to untie the knots we have made. However, if we all will just take time to reflect upon our oneness then we can begin to see how destructive we have been to our world and to each other. Understanding this destruction, we will come to see the need to stop it, and by stopping the harm we are now doing the wounds we have inflicted upon one another and our planet can heal. Once healed, we will then have the time and compassion needed to move toward a common future, and a clearer picture of ultimate truth.

We do not have to cast away all we now consider truth. All we have to do is analyze everything we think is true part by part, casting out what is error, admitting what we cannot know, and applying what is valid. If each human on earth would cast out one illusion a day, eventually we would all have a system of pure truth. Since there is only one truth, we would all be in harmony with each other and our world.

I have thought hard about the suffering and sickness present in our world, and suddenly one day it dawned upon me - it is here because humanity is not doing what it should with the resources it has. For each disease there is a cure. We could find them too, if we would stop cutting down the forests where the plants containing them reside, and use the money now devoted to killing each other to understand how to extract and use those medicines. Likewise, poverty could be put to death if we would all learn to be content with a little more than what we need, instead of hording our wealth to fulfill our wants.

The world is right now exactly what our choices have made it to be. Corrupt powers rule and direct our lives only because we let them. Humans want ease, simplicity, and prosperity, so crooked wise men step in and validate our selfish illusions. They give us answers that make us comfortable, and numb our minds with the pleasures we crave, so we never look deeper. Governments are made by people. If all the people would banish fear and realize government is fueled by the power they have given away, we could revolutionize our world. However, this requires all of us to be brave and not just a few; one person is no match for an army of millions.

Realize your mind is your own. Stop believing all the information authorities tell you, and seek to establish the truthfulness of their words. Let us destroy the walls of ignorance and evil that divide us. We can create a world where all are equal, where all can achieve their highest aspirations, and none have to suffer from want or disease. However, this requires each of us to devote ourselves to truth, and to see beyond our walls.

Do you have questions or comments? I would love to hear from you. Visit www.tmcoal.com to drop me a line, check for upcoming publications, or to get more copies of the one you just read.

www.ingramcontent.com/pod-product-compliance
Lightning Source LLC
Chambersburg PA
CBHW060921040426
42445CB00011B/733